Reputational Risk Management

Praise for Reputational Risk Management . . .

Reputations are at risk. For-profit and non-profit businesses spend their "lifetime" building a certain brand and reputation – and can lose the value of the brand and the strength of their reputation in a relatively short time – due to lack of planning.

No one exposes the dangers and explains the solutions better than Dr. Peggy Jackson. Her book "Reputational Risk Management," is a must for every CEO, CFO, CIO and corporate risk manager (or person charged with risk management duties).

The opening line of the preface sets the stage, "No organization ever envisions being embroiled in a crisis or scandal that will ever alter its good name and reputation." Well, it happens every day – are you prepared?

Christopher J. Boggs, CPCU, ARM, ALCM, LPCS, AAI, APA, CWCA, CRIS, Director of Education, Insurance Journal Academy of Insurance

Having worked with Peg Jackson for several years, one could not ask for a better risk manager to have in your corner. Her sixth sense is attuned to reputational risk management, a critical element in today's business environment.

Her newest book, *Reputational Risk Management*, is a must read for all business managers and owners; small, large or in between. They cannot afford to not know what they don't know. It can happen to them!

Devon Blaine, President & CEO, The Blaine Group, A Total Communications Agency and Crisis Management Firm

Reputational
Risk Management

Peggy M. Jackson, DPA, CPCU

Business Expert Publishing
Thomson, Georgia

Business Expert Publishing
The Business Expert Publisher™
P.O. Box 1389
Thomson, GA 30824

Published by Business Expert Publishing
Printed in the United States of America

Cover Design: Dave Blaker

First Edition

ISBN-13: 978-1-935602-02-6
ISBN-10: 1935602020

For Paul and Gemma

Table of Contents

Table of Contents

Step Three
Weaving Crisis Management Practices into the Organizational Fabric

Step Four
Staying on Track

Maximizing Value
How to Use this Book

No organization ever envisions being embroiled in a crisis or scandal that will forever alter its good name and reputation. Generally these events come as a bolt out of the blue. The damage is not simply confined to a product or some fleeting adverse publicity. There is real damage, probably permanent damage, to the company, nonprofit or academic institution's name, reputation, public trust and brand image. This is the type of catastrophe that is the worst nightmare of any executive. Reputational risk is often difficult to recognize or identify, but a company's good name and brand image are indeed very fragile. Unfortunately, in today's 24/7 media climate, the potential to generate adverse publicity is everywhere and the effects of an incident can be very long-lasting or even spell the demise of the organization.

This book is intended to be a primer on the nature of reputational risk and the steps every organization can take to reduce the potential for a reputational crisis and deal successfully when a crisis does occur. Anyone who uses Tylenol will know that a serious crisis does not mean that the company will implode. Tylenol survived because its management understood how to effectively deal with a reputational crisis.

What's Reputational Risk all about?

Organizations of all kinds, businesses, nonprofits and academic institutions can be irreparably harmed if their good name and image is no longer trusted by the public. The "brand" of their product/service can be permanently damaged by allegations of contamination, fraud or inability to deliver goods and services to customers.

Why should anyone care about reputational risk?

In today's business environment, catastrophic damage to an organization's brand and image can indeed cause it to implode. The former Big 5 accounting firm, Arthur Andersen, was virtually gone in a puff of smoke once they were indicted by federal prosecutors for their role in the Enron collapse. Arthur Andersen's clients, many of which were large corporations, simply were not willing to be associated with an accounting firm that was accused of facilitating fraud.

Who should read this book?

This book is for executives, board members and trusted advisors to businesses, nonprofits and academic organizations. The book is intended to help executives within these organizations as well as members of the board, IT professionals, public relations professionals, insurance professionals, financial professionals and attorneys. In short, anyone who is in a position to protect the organization's good name and public trust should read this book.

Features of the Book

- The topics discussed in each chapter apply to businesses, non-profits and academic institutions.

- The book presents solutions and techniques to deal with reputational risk can be readily scaled and adjusted to meet the needs of your organization. Size doesn't matter – you can scale the recommendations to fit your organizational needs.

- The book recognizes that today's companies, nonprofits and academic institutions have very similar business models that stretch across operational, managerial and governance areas.

Lessons learned from experiences in the nonprofit and academic world have applicability in the business world as well.

- All organizations are highly dependent on technology to the point that a serious interruption or compromise in the organization's IT system can have catastrophic consequences for the organization. Similarly, the use of technology as a means of communication including the internet, email, text messaging, cell phones, Blackberries, iPhones, iPods, Twitter, Facebook and the like are the norm in today's business, nonprofit and academic environments.

Structure of the Book – The Four Steps

The book is structured to walk the reader through four basic steps in learning about the nature of reputational risk and how to design a crisis management plan that is congruent with the organization's culture. Each of the chapters contains worksheets for the purpose of illustrating the points covered in the discussion. Copies of the worksheets are contained in the Appendix of the book for ease in use as the reader works on preparing a crisis management plan for his/her organization.

Step One – Reputational Risk: Learning about the Good, the Bad and the Ugly

Chapter 1 –Knowledge is Power: Learning about Common Sources of Reputational Damage. Chapter 1 introduces readers to the common sources of reputational risk and the role that organizational culture plays in fostering an environment that either facilitates crises, or works to reduce the potential for reputational calamities.

Chapter 2 –Lessons Learned from Responses to Reputational Crises. Often the most compelling lessons emerge from real-life experiences. Chapter 2 leads the reader through a series of reputational crises in business, nonprofit and academic institutions. The nature of a reputational crisis is just the beginning of the story. The manner in which the crisis is managed can spell the difference between survival and extinction.

Step Two – Designing and Executing a Crisis Management Plan

Chapter 3 - What are the Reputational Risks in Your Organization? Chapter 3 discusses the reputational risk elements that exist within every organization. The worksheets and checklists in this chapter will help the reader to determine which areas of vulnerability present a potential problem to the organization.

Chapter 4 - Preparing to Deal with a Crisis: The Plan. As was illustrated in Chapter 2, the resolution of a reputational crisis often hinges upon the quality of the planning that was done – or not done- in advance.

Chapter 5 - Action! Launching and Managing the Crisis Management Plan. Having a crisis management plan is only the first step in weathering a potential crisis of reputation. The quality of the execution of the plan is essential to its success.

Step Three – Weaving Crisis Management Practices into the Organizational Fabric

Chapter 6 –Training and Practice: Ensuring That Everyone Is Prepared To Take Action. Chapter 6 will guide readers through the design of an effective training plan. As was the case for a well-known brokerage in the World Trade Center on September 11th, having one's employees well-trained to deal with a crisis saves lives.

Step Four – Staying on Track

Chapter 7 - 10 Ways to Jumpstart the Process and Keep it Moving. All of the lessons learned in the chapters will not serve their purpose unless the reader begins to take action. The recommendations in this chapter will assist the reader in beginning the process as well as incorporating the best practices into the organization's daily operations.

Appendix and Resources

This section provides additional information on accessing risk management and business continuity planning and materials.

The Bottom Line

It's not a question of "if" but "when" an event occurs that has implications for your organization's reputation. Having a plan in place that everyone knows about and knows what to do and what NOT to do is essential for getting through the situation.

Your company, school or nonprofit's reputation is its most valuable asset. The value of your stock, access to capital, donations, strategic alliances and other intangible but indispensable elements all hinge upon the quality of the organization's reputation and good name. Don't let your organization be damaged because of a reputational crisis!

Step One

Reputational Risk: Learning about the Good, the Bad and the Ugly

one

Knowledge is Power!
Learning about Common Sources of Reputational Damage

Every business, nonprofit, or academic organization has the potential to be exposed to situations that can generate adverse publicity and result in damage to their reputation, brand and image. The headlines say it all:

- "Peanut Company Execs Refuse To Answer Lawmakers' Questions" (Peanut Corporation of America);
- "More Pet Deaths Expected in Tainted Pet Food Disaster" (Menu Foods);
- "Fry's Exec Dropped Millions on Gambling" (Fry's Electronics in Concord, CA)
- "Children's Hospital Exec Guilty of Child Porn" (Lucille Packard Children's Hospital at Stanford University in Palo Alto, CA).
- Woman Might Die From Eating [Nestlé]Cookie Dough, In Room 519 of Kindred Hospital (Las Vegas, NV) Linda Rivera can no longer speak.
- Bookkeeper Admits Embezzling from [novelist] Danielle Steele

The damage is not simply confined to a product or some fleeting adverse publicity. There is real damage, sometimes permanent damage, to the organization's name, reputation, public trust and brand image. Reputational vulnerability, or risk, is often difficult to recognize or identify, but an organization's good name and brand image are indeed very fragile. Unfortunately, in today's 24/7 media climate, the potential for the public to be exposed to adverse publicity about a business, nonprofit or academic organization is everywhere and the effects of an incident can be very long-lasting or, if egregious enough, even spell the demise of the organization.

How your organization deals with a crisis will be remembered long after the crisis has passed. In the Chinese alphabet, the character for the word "crisis" is also the character for the word, "opportunity." Your organization need not implode because of a reputational crisis if the response to the crisis inspires confidence and reinforces your organizational values. Many corporate, nonprofit or academic executives have no idea where to start. The inspiration for this book came from the need for this skill set.

The good news about dealing with reputational risk is that knowledge is power. This book will begin the process of learning about the sources of reputational risk, the lessons learned from reputational crises, what your organization's vulnerabilities are, and how to effectively plan for and deal with a crisis.

Common Sources of Reputational Crises

Reputational crises often emerge from a wide variety of areas including:

- Product liability issues including product recall.
- Board and/or senior management decisions.
- Adverse publicity arising from: Wrongful termination claims ; Sexual harassment claims; Work Comp claims and assertions of a dangerous workplace.
- Investigation of the firm by law enforcement or regulatory agencies.

- The other "brands" you are associated with, including strategic partners and non profits.

- Fraud

- Technology

- Outsourcing

- Respondeat Superior – actions that employees take while on the job.

Still other factors that render an organization vulnerable include "hot button" public relations issues relating to the environment or a political cause. Like any form of risk, it is impossible to totally eliminate the potential for a crisis. What is important is to recognize that these elements exist in virtually all organizations. The organizations that deal effectively with reputational risk recognize their vulnerabilities and are pro-active.

Basis for Reputational Risk

Product liability issues including product recall. The headline about the woman being in critical condition after eating Nestle cookie dough is typical of the incidents that generate adverse publicity about product safety. Other types of product liability publicity involved the contamination of pet food products that resulted in the deaths of countless pets. The fallout from these types of incidents goes beyond the simple product contamination or compromise. The lives of family members, friends and business associates are affected. Even if the product contamination only affects a limited number of people, the ripple effect can be enormous.

Board and/or executive management decisions. The sonic boom from the AIG board paying bonuses to executives in the wake of the Wall Street meltdown was heard across the planet. A "Pay Czar" was appointed to oversee and institute restrictions on executive pay and bonuses in light of AIG and other financial organizations receiving TARP money. Bonuses as part of the Bank of America merger with Merrill Lynch eventually led the Bank of America

CEO, Ken Lewis, to announce his retirement.

Adverse publicity arising from wrongful termination claims, sexual harassment claims, workers comp claims and assertions of a dangerous workplace. Adverse publicity and the threats of boycotts by interest groups can have a long-lasting negative effect on sales and opportunities for growth and expansion. Similarly, if OSHA or one of the state OSHA entities finds that the workplace is unsafe, particularly following a workplace injury event, then the ensuing adverse publicity can also damage the organization's reputation.

The other "brands" the organization is associated with including strategic partners and non profits. Ironically within weeks of the announcement of Ken Lewis's retirement, Bank of America withdrew its financial support of another very troubled organization, ACORN. Perhaps B of A didn't think it needed any more fodder for adverse publicity.

Fraud   Fraud is one of the most damaging means by which an organization's reputation can be damaged. The fact that the fraud occurred is damaging enough, but often the fraud is the result of poor or nonexistent internal controls, a corporate culture that enables these types of criminals to have free rein, and management that truly believes that as long as the insurance policy will pay for it, no measures need to be taken to clean up the organizational deficiencies. Chapter 3 includes an extensive discussion about fraud and how to clean up the organizational culture that fosters it.

Technology   The effective use and management of information technology is a core element in the way business is conducted today. Information technology includes, but is not limited to email services, databases, websites, electronic files, client information including credit cards, legal or medical files (for law firms and doctors' offices), donor information including credit cards, student information including grades, credit card information and medical information. All of these elements of IT are regulated in some form and all require a high level of security to protect the consumer, donor or student.

Outsourcing Vendors – Materials, Services, Staffing   The headline at the beginning of this chapter referring to novelist Daniele Steele's assistant's embezzling money also involved the assistant making a deal with the firm that Ms. Steele used to outsource her payroll. The assistant arranged for payroll payments that were more than she was entitled (www.cbs5.com). Clearly, Ms. Steele's problem regarding fraud wasn't just limited to her personal staff. The story is not necessarily inspiration for her next romance novel, but, hopefully for her taking a closer look at the integrity of her vendors.

Respondeat Superior   This legal principle states that the employer is responsible for employee behavior on the job, particularly if the behavior results in injury to another person. In the case of a You Tube video showing a Domino's Pizza franchise's employees behaving in an unsanitary manner, the fallout created a reputational crisis for the Domino Pizza corporate organization. Domino's Corporate stepped up to the plate by establishing a Twitter account. Corporate took responsibility for the incident even though the employees worked for one of their franchisees. They described what they were doing to take action to ensure that Domino's Pizza products were safe. They took the unusual step to set up a Twitter account because that appeared to be the media venue by which the story and video was being spread throughout the internet. Their actions to reassure the public of the safety of the Domino's menu succeeded (Horovitz, 2009).

Conversely, when the video surfaced showing the nonprofit, ACORN, volunteers giving advice to individuals posing as a pimp and prostitute, the Executive Director of ACORN went into full denial mode and blamed the media. ACORN's response to its reputational crisis continues to plague the organization's good name. Congress voted to withdraw funding and the Internal Revenue Service has severed its relationship with the organization's tax preparation services. Bank of American withdrew its corporate support (Hagerty, 2009).

Reputational Crises and Organizational Culture

Reputational crises frequently emerge from dysfunctional organizational cultures. Long before a reputational crisis appears, the seeds for the crisis have been sown and cultivated deep within the organization's culture So what is organizational culture? Organizational culture is a system of shared basic assumptions that helps people within the organization to cope with external forces, solve problems and pass along the learned methods for dealing with operational issues (Schein, 1992). In other words, the organization's culture describes its values, how it gets things done, what types of behaviors are allowed or not allowed, and the way it explains (or doesn't explain) problems to employees. Organizational culture is not "visible" per se, but it can often be sensed by the tone of the environment of the organization.

Examining an organization's culture will give clues as to why an organization has difficulty really solving problems. Why do the same problems keep coming back? Studying the attributes of an organization's culture assists in identifying the actual source of problems as well as crafting effective solutions. The actual source of the reputational crisis occurring today may be a set of assumptions or beliefs attributed to the organization's founder or to a management model used when the organization was first started.

Why Do Organizations Have Difficulty Really Solving Problems? Why Do The Same Problems Keep Coming Back?

Crises rarely emerge out of nowhere. With any of the reputational crises we will examine in this book, the clues were clearly in evidence long before the crisis erupted. For many organizations, problem-solving involves finding the quickest and cheapest solution to make the presenting problem go away. The presenting problem is what appears on the surface. Dealing with the presenting problem is not necessarily dealing with the genuine problem. This type of superficial response rarely is effective. Why? Organizations often do not recognize that serious problems exist until either a crisis erupts or some other disruptive incident occurs that fully grasps their attention.

Problems are often ignored because the organization's board and management tend to be more concerned about production deadlines, operational issues or short-term/long-term performance. In other words, executives are so focused on operational outcomes that they cannot summon the political will to make difficult decisions. Delving into difficult decisions may include taking the necessary steps to get at the root of the problem. For many organizations, Band-aids are quicker, easier and sometimes more politically correct.

One of the most effective ways to reduce the potential for reputational crises is to fully solve problems within an organization, particularly if these problems relate to financial controls, human resource management or operational areas such as manufacturing. The genuine problem may be systemic and require a much more extensive examination and remedy.

A quick fix will make the obvious symptoms go away but the underlying problem will still exist because the decision-makers did not take the time to dig deeper to identify the actual source of the problem. For example, if you had a laptop computer that kept crashing. You might try replacing the hard drive or operating system software, but what if that didn't work? You would probably arrange for a computer technician to determine the underlying mechanical cause of the problem and make the necessary repairs. Replacing the hard drive or operating system software are superficial approaches that probably would work well unless the laptop was experiencing a larger mechanical failure. Clearly, organizations are more complex than laptops. However, just as in the example of the laptop computer, superficial solutions applied to deep systemic problems do not render a satisfactory outcome.

Role of Organizational Culture and Citizenship in Reputational Risk

Learning to understand an organization's culture is much like peeling an onion, there are layers upon layers to peel back. Organizations aren't just the people that populate them, although the people are the face of an organization. From deep within organizations come the rules – written and unwritten – about how things are done, how problems are solved, and what's valuable. The unwritten rules exist because either everyone agrees with them, or everyone feels compelled for to obey them for reasons they often can't explain. For example, there may be an unwritten rule that says mistakes or errors should be hidden from supervisors. Other unwritten rules may preclude production supervisors from contacting executives about breakdowns of equipment or other mishaps after hours or on weekends.

Organizational culture is also reflected in the way newcomers are selected to join the organization in the capacity of administrator, employee, board member or other specific role. In any new job, there is generally a group of people tasked with showing the ropes to the new hire.

Often the unwritten rules come under the heading of how to get along around here. Some organizations are very open about how decisions are made, how ideas can bubble up and how grievances are settled. Others are more secretive. Information does not readily flow upward and downward within these types of organizations.

Probably the most powerful illustration of an organization's culture is centered in how normative behavior is molded. Normative behavior describes the types of behavior that are expected and considered acceptable within the organization. For example, the clerical employees in an office are expected to arrive on time at 8:30AM Monday through Friday, wear business attire, limit personal phone calls and take lunch at the time assigned to them. If they vary significantly in these behavioral expectations, there will probably be consequences imposed in the form of progressive discipline.

In understanding organizational culture, reward and punishment are not to be taken as entirely positive or negative. Consider the two words in terms of whether negative consequences are imposed by the organization for engaging in particular behaviors. Staff who do not show up for work and have not called in sick will probably have some sort of unpleasant consequences imposed for this behavior – reduction of pay for that week, assessing multiple sick days/ vacation days, or a letter of reprimand. However, depending on a manager's style, other negative behaviors such as failing to meet deadlines, failing to comply with new directives, or ignoring current rules might have no consequences imposed.

Conversely, some behaviors are discontinued, i.e. extinguished, because the person received insufficient positive reinforcement for the effort that s/he made. Consider the case of a staff member who worked long into the night to complete a report for the next day. If his/her supervisor does not show an appropriate level of appreciation, it is unlikely that the staff member will go to those lengths in the future. The behavior of working hard to make a deadline has been extinguished –generally for the rest of the time that the staff member works for that particular supervisor. Negative behavior can be extinguished as well if the immediate consequences are fast and sufficiently unpleasant to make a lasting impression. Whether or not any behavior is repeated is contingent upon the degree of positive or negative reinforcement that the person receives in response to the behavior.

An organization's culture supplies the reinforcing environment, values and beliefs to either reinforce or extinguish behavior. Every organization has a unique and irreplaceable culture that reflects its human dimension. As any organization becomes populated with toxic individuals at any level, the potential for dysfunction increases as does the potential for a reputational crisis.

Is Your Organization Dysfunctional?

Baseball great Yogi Berra was once quoted as saying, "It's amazing what you can see when you look." Most of the time dysfunction is not something that can be readily identified. A dysfunctional belief system is often at the root of organizational dysfunction. How often have you heard people in your organization say:

- It [a reputational crisis] will never happen to us!

- We don't need to do things like a business. We're a nonprofit serving poor people.

- No one would investigate us, sue us, or arrest any of our people for embezzlement, workplace violence or [some other action].

- We're a university – we don't have to do all of the things that corporations are expected to do.

- We work too long and hard as it is. We're not going to do more work.

- Our staff is not paid very well. I can't be expected to require high performance from them.

- I'm the founder and chief decision maker. I started this company and we'll do it my way. I know these clients better than anyone.

Dysfunctional belief systems within an organization can also be detected in the quality and quantity of output whether that is measured in terms of sales, manufactured products, enrollments or fundraising. How productive are staff members? Are reports and other deliverables produced on time? Are deadlines routinely missed? Performance issues relate to interpersonal interactions as well as to preparation of documents. How are clients and/or visitors treated when they enter the organization? Have clients or visitors complained that they were either ignored or treated in a callous manner? These types of complaints are not nuisance issues – take them seriously.

Appearance of Dysfunctional Organizations

The old adage you can't judge a book by its cover does not necessarily apply to work settings and the individuals who work there. Regardless of the individual's status within the hierarchy, the organization's credibility is diminished by the presence of individuals whose hygiene and mode of dress suggest that they do not understand that they are working professionals.

Similarly, the appearance of the organization's interior and exterior sets the tone for clients and visitors alike. The office housekeeping routine – or lack thereof – can signal serious dysfunction within an organization. If papers are piled high on desks and clutter abounds, that indicates a highly stressed organizational culture – and undoubtedly a significant number of errors based on the inability to manage documents.

Interpersonal behavior and Organizational Dysfunction

How do people in the organization treat each other? Body language and other nonverbal cues can provide clues to the source of organizational dysfunction. When the organization's leader arrives, do people scatter? Are board members permitted to give instructions to the rank and file staff?

How do people speak to each other in the organization? In dysfunctional organizations, there may be more overt displays of friction, such as staff shouting at each other – or management shouting at employees. Tone of voice, use of profanity and demeaning language are obvious clues of organizational difficulty. Whining or other adolescent-like speech patterns can hint at underlying morale problems – or it can signal a previously successful method of shirking responsibility. The more the staffer whines about being overworked, having no resources, no support, and no [fill in the blank], the less likely the recipient of the whining will insist on the deliverable.

More often than not, those who staff a dysfunctional organization will employ the default position of why they can't [provide the deliverable] rather than engage in meaningful discussion to develop a strategy which can deliver the goods. The more excuses, the more dysfunction.

Organizational Dysfunction and Executive Communication

Dysfunction in areas of communication can be observed in the way in which policies and procedures are explained, how changes in external environment are articulated, and how new policies/procedures that relate to current legislation are expected to be implemented.

Because knowledge is power, organizational leaders sometimes hoard whatever bits of information that they have. Fearing that by sharing this information their status within the organization might be compromised, these leaders do their best to ensure that only a select few have access to information. These individuals can go to great lengths to hide away information that has potentially important implications. Obviously, there needs to be a reasonable method for ensuring appropriate security for confidential information, but a culture of unnecessary secrecy in an organization is a huge red flag.

If the environment within the organization is one of secrecy – beware. Also beware of the gatekeepers that guard the secrets as these individuals are tasked with and rewarded for their unwavering attention to keeping secrets secret.

Organizational Dysfunction and the Lack Of Internal Controls

Many organization executives and board members believe that the concept of internal controls applies exclusively to finance and financial operations. Internal controls are necessary for the effective functioning of the board, Human Resources, IT, operations, and administration. The absence of internal controls is evidence not only of sloppy methods, it is also emblematic of a culture which does not have standards, or accountability. Not surprisingly, such a culture has a high probability of dysfunction if for no other reason than that of lack of accountability.

Organizational Dysfunction and Information Technology

The way in which technology is used, misused or ignored can signal dysfunction within an organization. One of the most common examples of dysfunction is the failure to stay current and to recognize that technology is an integral part of the internal control infrastructure. Sadly, many organizations fail to understand the degree to which they depend on technology. It is not just computers! The term technology relates to other important operational tools such as software, hardware, laptops and notebooks, PDAs, cell phones, voicemail, email and internet access. Failure to adequately manage this array of technology can not only indicate organizational dysfunction, it can also indicate a serious risk to the organization in the form of hackers, theft of confidential data, identity theft, potential for harassment of staff, donors or others, and other liability scenarios for the organization.

Organizational Dysfunction and HR

Human resource management holds many clues to the nature of organizational dysfunction. One of the most obvious indicators of organizational dysfunction is a permissive atmosphere that highlights a sense of entitlement on the part of the employees. Employees in these organizations are habitually late, dress in an unprofessional manner, and do not produce quality work. Employees are permitted to treat clients and visitors alike in a disinterested fashion – or even outright hostility. Employees are not trained or supervised. The organization fails to appropriately screen employees for sensitive work and handling confidential materials.

Another sign of organizational dysfunction is the volume of complaints regarding hostile work environment, sexual harassment or other dysfunctional behavior. Are there complaints about food or other personal items being stolen? Are office spaces orderly, or piled with paper and trash? Do staff members treat the organization's furniture, equipment and other materials with respect?

What is the tone of the furnishings inside staff members' work spaces? The furniture may be provided by the organization, but personal items including pictures, posters, slogan buttons and other signs can express –sometimes unmistakably- the disdain that the staff member has for the organization, a boss, or other targets within the organization.

Organizational Dysfunction and Public Trust

Public trust is one of the most important assets that an organization has – and at the same time it is one of the most elusive. Public trust is not something that can be shown to staff, clients, venture capital companies, nonprofit donors, shareholders or even members of the public. This fragile and subtle feature is the life breath of any organization. But like the life breath that sustains life itself, once it is compromised, the living organism is either damaged or dies. Companies that experience scandals or other crises do not always return to normal operation. Those organizations that fail to have a crisis communication plan or fail to be transparent or exhibit resentment of public inquiries about financial records are showing signs of dysfunction.

Organizational Dysfunction: Escalating a Molehill Problem into a Mountain Crisis

Most dysfunctional organizations do not understand how and why complaints by customers or employees can escalate into reputational crises or even litigation. The likely root cause of the crisis is that the aggrieved party was either ignored, their allegations dismissed as trivial, or they were treated with disrespect. The organization's executive team may not understand the techniques that can be employed to de-escalate a situation. In today's litigious environment, it is important for organizations to fully understand how to effectively address employee grievances and customer complaints in a manner that resolves the problem and retains the organization's good name and image.

Organizational Dysfunction and the Inability to Understand the External Environment

Keeping pace with current legislative and industry trends is more important than ever. The external environment is fraught with change – and this change is unlike that ever witnessed before. In the wake of Enron and other corporate scandals, the federal government is under pressure from the public to crack down on private sector and organization sector abuses. What has changed the way the private sector does business in the past decade has also changed the way nonprofits and academic institutions do business. Shareholder activism has paved the way for a new type of transparency in all organizations. Stakeholders, whether they are shareholders, donors, students, foundations or the public sector expect the organizations that they deal with to be trustworthy.

Organizational dysfunction is evident in management's failure to stay current with legislative changes as these relate to your type of organization, changes in public expectations and failure to stay current with industry issues. Denial of the importance of environmental scanning results in the failure to have everyone in the organization stay current on these issues and engage in routine professional development.

Role of Organizational Culture in Reputational Risk

A recurring theme in our discussion of the sources of reputational risk will be the contribution of the organization's culture to the event that triggers the reputational crisis. In virtually every example of a reputational crisis that is presented in this book, there is a connection to an element in the organization's culture. Sometimes it will be a level of dysfunction that is so high that it borders on toxic. Other examples will present an organizational culture that is stuck in a time warp. Still others will present an organizational culture that is firmly in denial that anything could possibly go wrong with their operations, relations with their clients or with their product.

By believing that a reputational crisis will never happen in your organization, you risk:

- Making front page news. Bear Sterns, Lehman Brothers and a host of Wall Street financial firms probably thought it would never happen to them. Kenneth Lay and Bernard Madoff probably never even dreamt that their firms would implode in horrific reputational crises.

- Inflicting permanent damage to your organization's brand and image that will either diminish or destroy the organization's competitive position. All organizations, including nonprofits and academic institutions, have brands and images.

- Losing sales at least in the short term as the details of the crisis unfold. This loss of sales may be so dramatic that your organization will not be able to secure financing or attract capital to fully resume operations and production.

- Exposing the organization to regulatory or criminal investigation.

Who's Watching Your Company? Your Nonprofit? Your University?

In today's 24/7/365 web-based media environment, a serious reputational crisis becomes news heard around the globe. Businesses, nonprofits and academic institutions are subjected to a higher level of scrutiny than ever before. Knowing who would be following the news of a crisis at your organization is important in crafting strategies to communicate with these stakeholder groups and in preparing information that would address their needs.

The Media

Public opinion of the corporate world and the nonprofit world is often influenced by the types of scandals it reads about in print or on the internet or hears dissected on cable television. Corporate scandals such as Enron, World Com or even Martha Stewart's drama were the source of news stories for months on end. ACORN, the American Red Cross and United Way affiliates across the country were just some examples of the pervasiveness of scandal-driven media coverage of nonprofits.

The world of higher education is not immune from this type of intense media attention. Any college, university or other academic organization who believe that the media couldn't possibly be interested in their operations need only review the almost daily coverage of the massacre at Virginia Tech. The coverage went on for weeks. The ever-present cameras, even the ones on a cell-phone can produce material for web sites such as Facebook and You Tube can make even the smallest story headline news if the timing is right. Media outlets such as CNN can arrive in virtually any location around the world within hours of a story.

Federal Regulatory Agencies and the Internal Revenue Service

A crisis that impacts an organization's reputation, brand and image attracts not only media attention, but can also attract the attention of industry regulators, OSHA and the Internal Revenue Service. No organization can afford to attract this type of scrutiny.

Watchdog Groups

Watchdog groups exist to keep tabs on the conduct of businesses, nonprofits and academic organizations. The purpose of these groups is generally to observe the organization's operations and interaction with the public for the purpose of loudly exposing actions that they deem harmful to their constituency, or the public at large. As with any sort of "watchdog" organization, some are more even-handed than others, generally based on their values and tenure.

The Better Business Bureau has long enjoyed a reputation of being a clearinghouse for businesses to ensure potential customers of the positive reputation of their members. The BBB gives ratings to firms based on a number of factors including how consumer complaints are handled.

The BBB's Wise Giving Alliance is a group that provides "consumer information" on nonprofits ostensibly to assist potential donors in identifying those nonprofits that are well-managed. The Alliance produces reports on national charities that specify whether or not an organization meets or does not meet the Standards for Charity Accountability. The reports do not rank or grade charities but rather seek to assist donors in making informed judgments about charities soliciting their support. In addition, the Alliance goes beyond standards to issue special alerts and advisories for individuals on topics related to giving.

For academic institutions, accreditation organizations, such as the Western Association of Schools and Colleges (WASC), the Council for Interior Design Accreditation (CIDA), and the Accreditation Bureau for Engineering and Technology (ABET), by virtue of their accreditation of an academic organization, grant their "stamp of approval" to its curriculum, governance and administration.

Who Else is Watching?

Bloggers   Bloggers may be watching your organization, but since they are not particularly accountable for their comments, you should not count on them to write accurately about your organization.

Clients, Customers, Donors, Students   Never underestimate the power of an annoyed customer, donor or student. Statistics note that this individual is likely to tell at least ten people about how unhappy s/he is with your product or service. That was before Yelp! or Yahoo or Google. Now an annoyed customer can tell the world about your shortcomings.

Vendors and Suppliers   Your vendors and suppliers are watching you closely –especially if they are sniffing financial problems. Recently a small chain of office supplies stores suddenly closed. One of the managers commented to the local radio station that he knew something was wrong because the vendors stopped shipping goods to the store.

Stockholders   Stockholders have become an important and highly vocal source of information on the well-being of their companies.

Potential strategic partners   Potential strategic partners are particularly cautious about who they deal with in today's business environment. Damage to your organization's reputation is likely to damage theirs as well.

Your organization has many reasons to handle any crisis will confidence and in a manner that inspires trust. Many people are watching you organization. The public has a long memory fueled by media images. Your organization's response can give them a reason to cheer for your success.

Summary

The source of reputational crises often lies deep within the organization's culture. Understanding your organization's culture and recognizing the source of deep-seated problems is essential in striving to reduce the potential for a reputational crisis.

While there is no guarantee that reputational crises can be completely eliminated, it is important to learn how to effectively deal with a reputational crisis While no one likes to see an organization permanently damaged because of missteps in handling a crisis, the instructive value of poorly-handled responses to reputational crises is significant. The responses to reputational crises presented in Chapter 2 will serve to further underline the role of organizational culture in the quality of a crisis response and will also serve to help readers understand the areas of organizational vulnerabilities presented in Chapter 3.

two

Lessons Learned
From Responses
to Reputational Crises

Hurricane Katrina became legendary not just because of the catastrophic damage this storm caused to New Orleans and the surrounding area. The federal, state, local and nonprofit response in the aftermath of destruction exposed shocking gaps in this country's emergency preparedness, and some might argue, in the integrity of some of the responding organizations. One of the most telling examples of ongoing reputational damage is the Federal Emergency Management Agency or FEMA. FEMA's Director at the time of Hurricane Katrina was Michael Brown. In light of FEMA's inept response, Mr. Brown's background was revealed as a political appointee with virtually no experience in emergency management. He was removed as principal disaster response coordinator under great pressure from the media and affected residents in New Orleans.

Coordination of disaster response was reassigned to Coast Guard ADM Thad Allen. Although replacing a civilian agency with the military in response to a disaster raised eyebrows, the Coast Guard had gained valuable public confidence by their rescuing over 30,000 people from rooftops and flooded buildings in New Orleans. The key word here is *confidence*. The Coast Guard's motto is *Semper Paratus*, meaning "always ready." Indeed they were in the wake of Katrina. Coast Guard helicopters had been staged on air bases just outside of the path of the hurricane in preparation for the rescue missions. ADM Allen, who was subsequently appointed

Commandant of the Coast Guard in 2006, was assigned to step into the public relations fray to coordinate response efforts and move the process forward. He was successful although New Orleans has still not fully recovered from this catastrophic event.

Despite the enormous expenditures on disaster relief, FEMA continues to experience reputational damage in the seemingly endless lawsuits over the toxic quality of trailers ostensibly supplied as temporary homes to residents of New Orleans. Since much of the housing in New Orleans is still not habitable, people continue to live in these trailers.

The lesson in this example centers on the way in which the Coast Guard's reputation as American heroes was reinforced based on their *response*. Consider the difference between the initial Coast Guard response which saved thousands of lives and the initial FEMA response which provided only minimal disaster response. The overall public perception may have contained some political considerations, but the results tell the story.

The public saw a U.S. President who was shocked by what he saw, a Mayor and Governor locked in political turmoil and a relatively new federal agency, the Department of Homeland Security, which was developing a still emerging mission within the federal government, but was the parent organization for FEMA and the Coast Guard. The public also saw a political appointee who was overwhelmed by the task of heading FEMA, and finally, the calm, steady know-how of a Coast Guard Admiral whose genius for logistics and strategy was first illustrated in the rescue of thousands trapped in lower Manhattan on September 11th. These were the faces and the actions that defined this country's response at that moment in time.

Hopefully, your organization will never have to endure anything as horrendous as Hurricane Katrina. When your employees, clients and stakeholders look back at your organization's response to a crisis, what do you want them to remember?

Reputational Crises Profiled In This Chapter

This chapter will profile reputational crises related to companies, nonprofits and an academic institution. The discussion of the crises will be structured to briefly summarize as follows:

- **The nature of the crisis** will be summarized.

- **The quality of the response** will describe how the organization chose to respond to the crisis.

- **What were the results?** The aftermath of the crisis will be profiled including business and economic fallout.

- **What were some of the underlying issues that triggered the crisis?** This discussion will address those issues which could have contributed to the crisis itself such as the organization's culture, corporate structure and executive mindset.

- **What can your organization learn from these reputational crises?** Lessons learned from these crises can be helpful in your organization's efforts to reduce the potential for reputational crises.

The organizations chosen as examples vary widely in terms of size, mission and industry. What they all have in common is the reputational aspects of the crises they encountered and the memorable characteristics of their responses. Clearly some organizations think faster on their feet than others. The quality of some of their responses was better than others, but all of these profiles should give the reader a sense that **none of the organizations ever really imagined the nature of the crisis that they ultimately faced.** The reputational crises profiled in this chapter relate to:

- **Arthur Andersen**. The accounting firm imploded following a federal indictment for obstruction of justice in the Enron prosecution.

- **Domino's Pizza**. The employees of a Domino's franchise make a crude video using the company's product and post it on the internet.

- **ACORN**. This grassroots social service organization lost funding from the federal government, foundations and the Bank of America following the release of videos showing their employees counseling a couple posing as a pimp and prostitute on how to establish a brothel.

- **American Red Cross**. This century-old nonprofit has had enough reputational crises to script a soap-opera. In the interest of space and time, the discussion will be limited to their Liberty Fund scandal.

- **Virginia Polytechnic Institute and State University (Virginia Tech)**. This academic institution made the headlines in 2007 for the horrific massacre of thirty-two (32) students and faculty at the hands of a deranged student.

The profiles of these organizations are as varied as the nature of the reputational crises covered in this discussion. Some of the organizations such as Dominos and Virginia Tech were successful at maintaining their reputation. Others, such as Arthur Andersen, could not withstand the blow. Still others, such as ACORN, remain mired in their reputational crisis with no resolution present at the time this book is going to print. The intent of the discussion is to present some important themes to the reader on the nature of reputational risk, the danger of denial, and the lasting effects of reputational damage.

Arthur Andersen

The nature of the crisis. The accounting firm Arthur Andersen was convicted in federal court of obstruction of justice in the Enron collapse. Among the factors that appeared to be crucial in the jury deliberations was the disclosure that an Andersen attorney instructed that her name be removed "from a file memo that disagreed with Enron's characterization of a $1 billion loss as 'non-recurring.'" Said prosecutor Andrew Weissman: "This is a perfect example of Arthur Andersen sanitizing the record so the SEC would have less information"(Thomas, 2002).

The quality of the response. Arthur Anderson appeared to address this crisis in the same reactive manner that they addressed previous crisis situations in which they were prosecuted for auditing misdeeds.

What were the results? Although the company threatened to appeal the obstruction of justice conviction, the firm closed its doors within three months of the verdict. Clients withdrew their business and employees left the firm.

What were some of the underlying issues that triggered the crisis? Over the previous fifty years the firm changed its corporate values changed from "putting reputation over profit" (Brown, Dugan, 2002) to values that fostered aggressive auditing practices and became mired in multiple instances of litigation in which the firm paid multi-million dollar settlements to plaintiff shareholders..

What can your organization learn from this reputational crisis? The organizational culture changed dramatically over the firm's 89 year history. The shift in organizational culture went from one that reinforced accounting industry standards and values to one that aggressively pursued profits seemingly at all costs. While an aggressive pursuit of profits might be consistent with industry standards in some fields, this approach, particularly when it involves breaking the law, is inconsistent with accounting industry values.

The lesson for private, nonprofit and academic organizations is that dramatic shifts in organizational values that do not embrace parallel compliance practices will damage the organization. In other words, if your organization chooses to change its corporate values, leaders must ensure that the new values are within the boundaries of the laws and regulations that apply to your organization.

Domino's Pizza

The nature of the crisis. Two employees of a Domino's Pizza franchise filmed an unsanitary preparation of a pizza violating other health-code standards while a fellow employee provided narration and posted it online. The two were charged with delivering prohibited foods. Domino's Pizza Corporate faced a public relations crisis as more than a million people viewed the video on YouTube. References to it were in five of the twelve results on the first page of Google search for "Dominos," and discussions about Domino's had spread throughout Twitter (Clifford, 2009).

A spokesperson indicated that the company was preparing a civil lawsuit. "Even people who've been with us as loyal customers for 10, 15, 20 years, people are second-guessing their relationship with Domino's, and that's not fair" (Clifford, 2009).

The quality of the response. Domino's Corporate Headquarters stepped in and set up a Twitter Account to combat the adverse publicity. "Domino's first responded on consumer affairs blog The Consumerist, whose activist readers helped track down the store and employees who made the video. Then it responded on the Twitter site where talk was mounting" (Horovitz, 2009). The Corporate response was able to gain traction because it went to the source of the information on the video, namely the web. Clearly given the number of people who watched the YouTube video, that's where the source of any reputational damage would be. Domino's Corporate understood that in order to restore its credibility it needed to communicate with this customer contingency via Twitter.

What were the results? Domino's was able to preserve its customer confidence and good image because of its swift response including pressing charges against the franchise employees. A more subtle but important result of the crisis was the realization that "Nothing is local anymore," Domino's spokesman Tim McIntyre says. "That's the challenge of the Web world. Any two idiots with a video camera and a dumb idea can damage the reputation of a 50-year-old brand." Domino's is also considering banning the use of videos in its stores (Horovitz, 2009).

What were some of the underlying issues that triggered the crisis? The structure of a corporation with franchise outlets exposes the parent organization to situations like Domino's video. Franchise owners hire and supervise their employees. Whatever the employees do reflects back on the parent company. The franchise agreement can specify what type of training is required, but depending on the nature of the franchise agreement, Corporate may have limited authority on hiring and firing employees.

Corporate culture in a franchise operation becomes very localized. The corporation may have an organizational culture that promotes a high quality of professional behavior, but the parent organization is not in a position to supervise a local franchise. Thus the corporate culture is whatever the franchise deems it to be. In this situation, there appeared to be very little training and/or supervision in this particular franchise.

What can your organization learn from this reputational crisis? News about a company or an incident travels at lightning speed on the web. Companies should monitor social sites to ensure that events or conversations similar to the Domino's incident are not posted or reported. It would be prudent to assign an employee to monitor these sites. Domino's corporate headquarters responded quickly and in a manner that communicated directly with the constituency using these social sites.

"Educate workers. It's important that all employees have some media and social-media training, says Ross Mayfield, co-founder of Socialtext, which advises companies on new media" (Horovitz, 2009). "Set clear guidelines. Companies must have clear policies about what is allowed during working hours — and what isn't, Doll says. "It won't prevent everyone from breaking the rules, but at least they'll know what the rules are" (Horovitz, 2009).

Association of Community Organizations for Reform Now (ACORN)

The nature of the crisis. This grassroots nonprofit organization has been plagued by allegations of voter registration fraud, embezzlement. In the summer of 2009 two filmmakers posing as a pimp and prostitute secretly videotaped "ACORN employees in four of the agency's offices suggesting or condoning a series of illicit actions as the couple sought advice on setting up a brothel with underage women" (Frieden, 2009).

The quality of the response. Bertha Lewis, CEO of ACORN, responded with a stunning mixture of hubris, denial and refusal to take responsibility for the actions of her organization. Ms. Lewis's default position was that the videos were a political dirty trick. If the ACORN employees refused to assist the alleged pimp and prostitute, there would be no story.

What were the results? Once the video was released via the web, federal funding as well as private funding from foundations and Bank of America was withdrawn. The U.S. Census Bureau dropped ACORN as a partner for the 2010 Census (Hagerty, 2009). The Louisiana Attorney General launched an investigation into allegations of tax violation and obstruction of justice in October 2009. The preliminary results of the investigation show that Dale Rathke, brother of the founder of ACORN, embezzled somewhere between $1million to $5 million from the organization. The exact figure is in dispute as the investigation is ongoing (Robertson, 2009).

If the ACORN employees and volunteers had used common sense, they never would have counseled *anyone* to engage in illegal activity. The individuals posing as a pimp and prostitute went to several ACORN offices and were removed in at least one instance. The staff in another ACORN office called the police because the couple wanted advice on how to bring underage children into the United States for prostitution. Clearly not every ACORN chapter is managed as poorly as the corporate headquarters. However, the organization now appears to be in a serious reputational crisis.

What were some of the underlying issues that triggered the crisis?
As the ACORN crisis unravels it appears that a number of issues contributed to the triggering of the crisis. The organizational structure appears to be something of a patchwork of sub-organizations and the organizational culture appears to be highly dysfunctional at best. ACORN has had significant management and governance problems in recent years. The founder, Wade Rathke, was forced out of leadership and replaced by Ms. Lewis whose background, ironically, is in the theater industry.

Although the organization appears to be a lightning rod for political controversy, it appears that many of their problems are self-inflicted. The staff does not appear to be well-trained, nor does the corporate headquarters appear to understand the significance of having and executing an effective crisis communication plan.

What can your organization learn from this reputational crisis?
Although at this point there is no resolution to the ACORN crisis, some preliminary lessons can be considered.

- Select people to lead your organization whose experience and background are appropriate to the needs of the position. Your organization's reputation will be ill-served by a spokesperson who is neither trained in media relations, nor trained to serve in executive management.

- Establish guidelines for the delivery of goods and services. Train employees to understand that the quality of their service and customer relations directly impact the organization's bottom line. If your company, nonprofit or academic institution offers counseling or services of that nature, the employees need to be carefully trained and vigorously supervised.

- Prepare and practice an effective crisis communication plan. Your organization's Designated Spokesperson needs to be an intelligent, articulate and credible individual who has received training in media relations. Chapters 4 and 5 will present more information on the design and execution of this important role.

American Red Cross

The nature of the crisis. Following the September 11th attacks on New York and Washington, the American Red Cross (ARC) launched a phenomenally successful fundraising drive. The Red Cross claimed that all of the monetary donations were going to be used to assist the surviving families of people who were killed in the attacks. The Red Cross President, Dr. Bernadine Healy, established the "Liberty Fund" to consolidate these donations.

The structure of the Liberty Fund was intended to shield a closely guarded Red Cross secret. Historically, money collected from disaster-related fundraising efforts was put into the overall budget of ARC Disaster Services. Traditionally, there was never any assurance to the American public that all of the money collected for a specific disaster would be used exclusively for that purpose. The intent was to utilize whatever the current "disaster" was as a means of raising funds to support future disaster scenarios. Red Cross "insiders" were outraged that Dr. Healy, who was a relative newcomer to the Red Cross and thus an "outsider," chose to segregate the enormous sums being donated as a result of the September 11th attacks. As pressure began to mount to integrate the Liberty Fund donations with the rest of the disaster relief funds, Dr. Healy delayed the payment of gifts to the victims' families. (Jackson, 2006).

The quality of the response. The Red Cross refused to take any action until Congress intervened. The September 11th victims' families complained to Congress and soon Senator Charles Grassley(R Iowa), then Chair of the Senate Finance Committee, took action. The Red Cross changed its position and stated that all of the Liberty Fund monies would be distributed to victims' families (Jackson, 2006).

What were the results? The media coverage of the complaints from the September 11th victims' families raised public awareness that 1) the funds from the Liberty Fund were not being distributed as advertised and 2) there was significant pressure being put on Dr.

Healy by the ARC Board of Governors to integrate the money into the overall Disaster Services funds. Eventually, some of the families did receive cash gifts, but only after Congressional inquiry and continuing media coverage. The Red Cross Board of Governors retaliated by forcing Dr. Healy to resign as ARC President (Jackson, 2006).

What were some of the underlying issues that triggered the crisis? The marginal quality of the internal controls of the American Red Cross at the corporate and local chapter levels have been a continuous source of problems for the organization. Fiscal mismanagement was something of a common occurrence. As part of his investigation of the Liberty Fund, Senator Grassley learned that the Red Cross board had ignored the embezzlement of $1 million by Hudson County, New Jersey, chapter officials. Although Dr. Healy attempted to have the Chapter Executive fired, she was stymied by the Board of Governors. Grassley determined that other issues which surfaced included the lack of accountability of chapters for annual performance; a reluctance of [Red Cross] Headquarters to exercise hiring and firing authority over chapter executives; and a tendency of Headquarters to relegate its authority to an advisory role as it relates to chapters. The Red Cross had limited organization-wide systems to ensure compliance (Jackson, 2006).

What can your organization learn from this reputational crisis? The Liberty Fund crisis was one component among several concurrent crisis scenarios occurring at the American Red Cross National Headquarters during that timeframe. The overriding theme of all of the crises was a failure to tell the truth and a failure to ensure that donations were being used as the donors intended.

One of the most significant elements in reputational risk management is the value of institutional integrity. Your organization, regardless of the circumstances of a crisis, must tell the truth and must be transparent. Your clients, customers, donors (for nonprofits), students and families (for academic institutions) are counting on you to tell them the truth! It's just that simple. Waiting until a member of Congress and the media force you to tell the truth will damage your reputation.

Virginia Polytechnic Institute and State University (Virginia Tech)

The nature of the crisis. On April 16, 2007 a deranged student shot and killed thirty-two (32) students and faculty members on the Virginia Tech campus. The student, Seung Hui Cho, shot and killed two students in a dorm and then went on to a classroom building where he gunned down thirty students and faculty in one of the most horrific incidents in memory.

The quality of the response. The campus police and local law enforcement were hampered by communications issues and/or devices to signal an emergency on campus. The processes for alerting the campus and the media to an emergency were very protracted. The Virginia Tech campus police had the authority to send an emergency message; they did not have the technical means to do so. Only two people, the associate vice president for University Relations and the director of News and Information, had the codes to send a message. The police could not access the alerting system to send a message. The police had to contact the university leadership on the need and proposed content of a message (Report of the Virginia Tech Review Panel, 2007).

What were the results? Following the massacre, the State of Virginia convened a blue-ribbon panel to investigate the incident. The panel determined that current federal and state privacy policies were hampering the ability to identify and treat troubled students. There were serious gaps uncovered in the university's emergency preparedness and response (Report of the Virginia Tech Review Panel, 2007).

What were some of the underlying issues that triggered the crisis? Issues that contributed to the crisis included the community and the university's lack of assertive policies for dealing with troubled students. The gunman had been under court order to undergo psychiatric treatment, but no one checked to ensure that the student complied with the order (Report of the Virginia Tech Review Panel, 2007).

The institution's organizational culture focused heavily on ensuring the privacy of students without taking into consideration the welfare of the overall student population. Several members of the faculty raised concerns about Cho's mental state, but their concerns were ignored by the administration.

The Panel found that the Virginia Tech Emergency Response Plan was deficient in these areas:

- The Plan was out of date – contained information that was not current.
- Did not include provisions or training to deal with a shooting scenario.
- Protocols for sending an emergency message in use on April 16th were cumbersome, untimely and problematic when a decision was needed as soon as possible.
- Police did not have the capability to send out an emergency message – had to await the deliberations of the Policy Group of which the police were not members. Policy group had to be convened to decide whether to send a message to the university and to structure its content.
- No security cameras were in place in the dorms or anywhere else on campus (Report of the Virginia Tech Review Panel, 2007).

What can your organization learn from this reputational crisis?
The massacre at Virginia Tech is a particularly horrendous example of **workplace violence**. No one at the university appeared to anticipate that an event like this could ever take place. No one in the student population, particularly Cho's roommates, appeared to be even aware of the stockpile of weapons he was storing in his room. Thirty-two people paid the ultimate price because a university administration chose to hide behind policies and regulations rather

than take action to deal with a mentally ill student.

The institution did not have a means of alerting the entire campus to shelter in place, or to alert them via text messages or email or by putting a message on their computer screens. Based on the Review Panel's report the institution certainly did not ever engage in shelter-in-place exercises or even in exercises which would alert the entire campus to an emergency situation.

There are two important lessons to take away from this tragic example. The first is that workplace violence can and will happen. It doesn't need to make sense particularly if the perpetrator is mentally ill. Despite what appears to be an abundance of laws at the federal and state levels, mentally ill people still seem to be able to obtain weapons. The second lesson is that there is no substitute for a well-crafted crisis management plan that is practiced routinely and is understood by everyone in your organization. Chapters 4, 5 and 6 will present a generic crisis management plan, strategies for activating the plan and a training agenda to ensure that your employees are prepared to deal with emergency situations.

Lessons Learned

The examples of reputational crises presented in this chapter illustrate the degree to which a crisis scenario can skyrocket into national news. The organizations profiled varied dramatically in their responses to the crises. Some organizations, such as Virginia Tech, survived and went on to champion changes in dealing with workplace violence within their own industry (academia). Others, such as Arthur Andersen, imploded in a puff of smoke. No organization can ever predict the exact nature of a crisis scenario, but the following themes should be considered as your organization begins work on designing a crisis management plan.

Denial is not a planning strategy. Crisis scenarios will still occur even if you don't plan for them. The Virginia Tech shootings were a shocking example of workplace violence. This is not a topic that many organizations like to discuss or prepare to address. Similarly, the topic of fraud or financial mismanagement is not one that organizations generally are eager to address. Both scenarios can destroy an organization if the crisis management response is not credible.

The organization's corporate headquarters needs to be able to respond quickly. Companies, nonprofits and academic institutions with branch offices or franchises need to take special care to ensure that these sub-organizations are fully prepared to deal with a crisis situation. The Domino's Pizza franchise whose employees uploaded the video did not appear to have a plan to deal with a crisis. Fortunately Domino's Pizza Corporate Headquarters did have a plan and at least one person who understood how to communicate with its array of constituencies. If Domino's executive management had not quickly created a Twitter account to combat the negative publicity based on workers' behavior, the company's reputation could have suffered even more damage.

Clients and corporate sponsors will flee from companies/nonprofits mired in scandal. Arthur Andersen imploded almost instantaneously when they were convicted of obstruction of justice in the case involving their audits of Enron. Nonprofits such as ACORN have funding sources that go beyond individual donations such as federal and corporate funding. The House of Representatives voted to withdraw funding for Acorn as did the Bank of America.

The value in having effective crisis management and crisis communication plans. Effective crisis management and crisis communication plans would have been very beneficial in all of the examples cited in this chapter. Despite the seeming lack of crisis management and crisis communication plans, some of the organizations such as Domino's and Virginia Tech were able to preserve their reputations. Others, such as Arthur Andersen were not. Time will tell if nonprofits such as ACORN and the American Red Cross will successfully weather their crises with their reputations intact.

Summary

The organizations and crises profiled in this chapter represent a wide variety of scenarios and responses. In each case the organization's vulnerabilities served to further ignite the crisis at hand and turn what might have been a manageable situation into an event that had a prolonged life in the media and perhaps in the minds of the organization's customers, regulators and other stakeholders. Chapter 3 will discuss the ways in which your organization can examine its areas of vulnerability and perhaps take action to mitigate a situation that has potential to erupt into a reputational crisis.

Step Two

Designing and Executing
a Crisis Management Plan

three

Reputational Risks
In Your Organization

The examples of reputational damage in Chapter 2 were, to some extent, self-inflicted. Had the organizations been aware – or were willing to do something about – the areas of reputational risk within their structure, could the results have been less destructive? A common theme in the examples presented in Chapter Two is the lack of understanding about those elements that generate reputational risk in an organization. Being pro-active about reputational risk vulnerabilities will not guarantee that the organization will be exempt from adverse incidents. However, being pro-active about reputational risk vulnerabilities will give the organization a head-start in preparing to deal confidently with these occurrences. This chapter will help you to identify those areas of your organization's organization, structure, governance, management and operations that could trigger a reputational crisis. By examining those areas of potential vulnerability, you can take steps to reduce the potential reputational risk and the likelihood that an adverse event would occur. Being aware of the vulnerabilities specific to your organization will also help to shape the Crisis Management Plan outlined in Chapter 4.

How an organization handles a crisis will be remembered long after the crisis has passed.

Discovering the Sources of Potential Reputational Crises

As we discussed in Chapter 1, reputational crises can stem from a myriad of sources – some present within the organization and some external including association with an organization that is experiencing a reputational crisis. As we observed in Chapter 2, many organizations suffer reputational crises because there was very little introspection to identify the areas of organizational vulnerability. Although it is not an efficient use to time to try to identify every possible scenario in advance, this chapter will present those areas that often cause reputational problems. To streamline the discussion, the issues will be presented in this manner:

- **Source of Potential Reputational Crisis.** Vulnerability sources emerge from all components of the organization. The intent in this section is to identify those areas that are most common culprits in reputational risk crises.

- **Description of the reputational risk issues.** For the purpose of this discussion, only the most likely issues will be presented. As you examine your organization for vulnerabilities, recognize that there may be some issues that are unique to your organization.

- **Possible steps to mitigate the risk.** These depend on the organization and the industry, but serve to describe possible methods. The discussion presents some examples of steps used to mitigate risk. Be aware that your organization might need to apply other risk mitigation treatments. Your trusted advisors are important sources of information in determining the most effective risk mitigation strategies.

Worksheets For Each General Area of Reputational Risk

Worksheets for each area of Reputational Risk may be downloaded at www.pegjackson.com

The sources of potential reputational crisis are grouped in terms of generic organizational components including governance and management, human resources, operations, IT and Cyber Risks, fraud and workplace violence.

Governance and Management

The management and governance of any organization sets the tone for its operations. As we saw in Chapters 1 and 2, common elements in reputational risk crises were the attitudes and actions of senior management, and by extension, the board of directors. Today's business environment for companies, nonprofits and academic institutions emphasizes a new governance paradigm in which boards are responsible for everything that goes on within an organization. This expectation by regulators, shareholders and the public has played out in a number of recent reputational crises.

Checklist for Governance and Management

- Are board members furnished with financial statements and other materials well in advance of the board meetings?
- Is an agenda prepared and followed for each board meeting?
- Are minutes kept for each board meeting?
- Do board members come to the meetings prepared to discuss the issues on the agenda?
- Is there a specific decision-making process, i.e., specific length of time for discussion followed by a vote?
- If a topic needs to be deferred for a vote at a later date, are there specific steps and/or information that will be gathered so that the board can take a vote when the topic is revisited?
- Are board members required to complete a Conflict of Interest letter on an annual basis?

- Does the board have specific protocols to handle conflicts of interest as they occur?

- Are board members fully briefed (usually at an orientation) about their fiduciary obligations?

- Are board members required to sign a Code of Ethics, and are they held accountable for conducting themselves in accordance with the code?

- Are board members briefed on the nonprofit's mission and how that mission is affected by board decisions?

- Are board members briefed on the correlation between their decision-making and their fiduciary obligations as these impact the nonprofit's mission?

- Are board members briefed on the correlation between the quality of their performance and the nonprofit's mission?

Some common problem areas include:

Executive management reacts negatively when receiving bad news from subordinates and business units. This results in a culture that avoids reporting bad news. When the managers in an organization are reluctant to share bad news upward, the organization will not be able to react in time to deal with a crisis situation.

The organization either does not have or does not enforce a Conflict of Interest Policy for its board and management. Failure to have and enforce a Conflict of Interest Policy sets the tone for possible fraudulent activities and behaviors. All members of the board and members of the executive, senior and middle management, particularly those involved in financial and procurement functions should be required to disclose real or potential conflicts of interest in writing on an annual basis.

Management and the board have not reviewed and strengthened the organization's internal controls, particularly as these relate to financial operations One of the most common comments by executives in the wake of an incident of embezzlement or fraud is that they never saw it coming and had absolute trust in the employee because s/he had been with the organization for so many years. Of course they stayed – they could get away with stealing! In the discussion on fraud in this chapter, we will examine how the failure to provide aggressive oversight of internal controls contributes to a culture of deception.

Fraudulent financial reporting at any level and in any form is either ignored or tacitly tolerated. How could fraud be tacitly tolerated? By people who have no idea what they are looking at when they review the financial statement. Board members and executives who don't really understand financial reports and cannot spot negative trends or suspicious entries are tacitly tolerating fraud.

Loans and salary advances are permitted for board members and executives. Many non profits and small businesses routinely make loans or financial advances to board members and employees. This is a very dangerous practice for any organization and can result in some very negative publicity.

Reports of waste, fraud and abuse are either ignored or punished. From Enron to the University of California in San Francisco, the tales of whistleblowers being punished continues. Dr. David Kessler, former head of the Food and Drug Administration, was fired in 2007 as the Dean of the UCSF Medical School after he cited financial irregularities. Recently the US Senate Finance Committee and Sen. Charles Grassley pressured the university to conduct a financial review of its San Francisco Campus (Chronicle of Higher Education, December 8, 2009). The audit by Price Waterhouse Coopers is ongoing as this book goes to print.

The organization's business risks are hidden from discussion with the board of directors. If the organization's culture is one that discourages sharing of bad news, then the likelihood that the board will be kept fully apprised of business risks is very low.

Business risks apply to all organizations, not just private sector ones. Nonprofits and academic institutions take business risks when they add new programs or expand their current facilities. Hiding the degree of the risk or the aspects of the risk that would trigger red flags is suspect behavior.

Human Resources

The Human Resources division of any organization is tasked with administering and enforcing a myriad of policies and protocols. Employees are provided with their first understanding of the organizational culture by means of their interaction with HR.

Some common problem areas include:

Dysfunctional hiring, supervisory and termination practices. Hiring employees is a tricky business in today's environment. When incidents of fraud or criminal behavior come to light, often the individual was hired without having gone through background, credit or criminal screening.

Lack of grievance procedures for issues other than waste, fraud and abuse.

Employees have been known to go to the media to expose workplace conditions or wrongful supervisory allegations because they do not have an effective system within the organization to file grievances for issues other than waste, fraud and abuse. Many of the grievances that find their way to the media could have been resolved quietly within the organization had there been an effective grievance system in place.

- **Employees feel free to talk to the media.** When employees are on the job, there needs to be an absolute rule that all media inquiries are referred to the designated spokesperson. Employees either don't realize or don't care that at the moment they are on camera, they become the "face" of the organization. Who acts as the "face" of the organization is management's call – not the employees.

- **Sexual harassment and other forms of fraternization are ignored.** One wonders if CBS's entertainment division has a policy on sexual harassment or fraternization. Even if they do, clearly their high profile employees like David Letterman appear to be exempt from accountability. Only time will tell if this scandal will have any effect on ratings. However, companies, nonprofits and academic institutions cannot afford to have events of this nature tarnish their reputations.

- **Work Comp claims continue to increase in frequency and severity.** If the premium for your Work Comp policy rises every year, it might be because of the experience modification, which is the annual record of claims for injuries or workplace-related illnesses. Workplace safety and possible investigation by regulatory agencies such as OSHA can trigger a reputational crisis.

- **Travel and other reimbursable claims that appear to be inflated or inaccurate.** Extensive incidences of fraud generally begin with small things such as inflated travel claims or requests for reimbursement that are not documented with receipts. Although this may appear to be trivial, it is the thin edge of the wedge. Once a person tests the system in this manner and determines that there are no consequences, the scope of the fraud expands.

- **Employees are issued company credit cards for travel and other work-related expenses.** The *San Francisco Chronicle* headline read, "San Francisco Schools Head Uses District   Credit as Own" (SF Chronicle, October 4, 2009). The City's School Board President used her district-issued credit card to charge over $15,000 for personal use. In today's business world this sum can be dismissed as small change. In this instance, however, the city's School Board had recently cut school budgets dramatically. This new instance of seemingly hypocritical behavior on the part of the head of the school board further aggravated parents and teachers and yet again put this troubled school system in a negative spotlight.

If your school organization does not have a Grievance Policy, consider using the following checklist to develop a plan.

Checklist for the grievance policy:

Name

Are you a: (check one)

- Visitor
- Customer
- Employee
- Member of the public/neighborhood
- Other

Nature of the complaint:

Names of staff members involved:

Names of any other individuals involved:

Were there injuries? If so, describe the injuries?

Was there property damage or theft? [Describe the property, give the value of the property and describe damage if applicable.]

Checklist to investigate a grievance complaint:

Chief Investigator [name and title]

Assisting in the investigation [Give names/titles]

Date of the Report:

Date that complaint was received:

Date that investigation commenced:

Date that investigation concluded:

Law Enforcement contacted? Yes_____ No_____

Summary of the complaint [maximum of 250 words – approx]

Findings

Recommended Action Steps

Fraud

Fraud can be one of the most destructive sources of reputational damage. Fraud and fraudulent activities don't simply happen overnight and can seriously injure your organization's reputation because the fraud points to defective internal controls. Fraudulent activities can attract the attention of the media, law enforcement and regulators. Potential clients, shareholders and associates read these reports and could become disenchanted with your organization. Depending on the scale of the fraud, the resulting damage could seriously affect the financial integrity of the organization as well as leave it open to criminal charges.

An instance of serious fraud could destroy the organization's ability to obtain insurance coverage or secure another round of venture capital funding. Fraudulent activities might not be reimbursed unless the organization has secured the appropriate insurance coverage. However, even if the organization has proper insurance coverage that does not guarantee that the insurance company would be willing to pay out on multiple claims.

Here are some examples of the reasons that fraudulent activities take place within companies, nonprofits and academic institutions:

- **The organization's culture.** If the company, nonprofit or university denies the possibility of their employees committing fraud, or transforms employees into martyrs, the potential for fraud increases. How many times have you heard people in nonprofits or academic institutions say, "We work so hard here for so little money." That should be a red flag! This is not to say that businesses are immune to fraud – far from it. However, the risk for fraud grows exponentially when the organization's culture suggests that management is clueless.

- **A business owner and/or management team that are asleep at the wheel.** How often do we hear stories about fraud committed at organization only to learn that the owner and senior management knew nothing about it and suspected nothing. That's one of the most important reasons why senior management needs to lead the way in talking about fraud and in instituting and enforcing anti-fraud measures.

- **Management assertion that "It's not a problem, we have insurance."** In a number of cases of fraud reported in the media, the organization's designated spokesperson's only comment was "we have insurance." They did not indicate that internal controls were going to be strengthened, or that all systems related to finance, operations or the like would be examined. They clearly don't think that there's any need for examination or modification – they have insurance! Of course one might like to be a fly on the wall when they receive their next bill for their insurance premiums – or the cancellation/ non-renewal notice.

- **Lack of Consequences.** Individuals who engage in fraudulent activities want to steal and either don't believe they will be caught or believe that there will be few if any consequences for their behavior. If they work for an organization that believes that employees are not capable of fraud, or that employees are martyrs, or there's no need to worry because the organization has insurance...then these potential fraudsters have no need to fear.

- **The opportunity for fraud to take place.** In other words, there are weak or nonexistent internal controls which provide the opportunity to engage in fraudulent activities. Other occasions can include access to petty cash, or other assets that are quickly converted to cash.

- **Weak or nonexistent internal controls.** It's easier to cover one's tracks when there are no policies, procedures or internal controls.

- **Unrestricted access to electronic databases and online checking.** Often electronic records will need to be altered to cover the fraud. Individuals who have access to sensitive databases are in a position to set up sham accounts and issue checks to themselves.

Portals to Fraudulent Behavior

People who engage in fraudulent behavior look to find the easiest targets within an organization. Some examples of portals to fraud include:

Travel claims not processed in a consistent manner.

Reimbursements subject to arbitrary measures. Senior management not required to provide the same level of documentation for a reimbursement claim as would a member of the rank and file.

Unauthorized use of debit/credit cards. Many organizations permit senior executives to use debit/credit cards issued to the organization.

Unauthorized use of organization accounts with specific vendors. Organizations need to have a means by which charges must always be linked to a verified project number.

Invoices from consultants and/or other vendors can be modified to cover for fraudulent activities.

Check disbursements and reconciling bank statements should be segregated duties.

Loans, gifts, bonuses and perks to executives. Organizations often agree to loans and gifts to executives as incentives or as rewards for performance. Businesses, particularly if there is a corporate board, are under much more scrutiny in terms of the way in which executive compensation packages are approved. Family-owned businesses could have additional problems in the blending of their business and personal relationships.

Expense accounts and travel claims. Financial misappropriation often is hidden in transactions involving expense accounts and travel claims.

Travel Claims Worksheet
Travel claims submission process:
Travel claims are submitted

- On a specific form designed by the organization

- Within the authorized timeframe for submission. Late submissions require a signature by a Vice President or above.

- Necessary information:

    - the name of the employee,

    - dates traveled,

    - purpose of travel,

    - listing of expenses and

    - original documentation – travel authorization form signed by supervisor.

- Travel claims will not be paid unless the form is completed correctly and there is supporting documentation for all expenses.

- If the travel claim includes reimbursement for meals, the purpose of the meal and the names of the guests are included in the documentation.

- Receipt for parking and/or mileage - If parking or transportation to the airport is an authorized expenditure, the travel claim also needs to have either a receipt for parking or a mileage listing.

- The travel expense policy includes a list of authorized expenditures. Any expenditures submitted that are not included as authorized expenditures on the list must be approved by the CFO before they can be reimbursed.

Senior management will make random and unannounced examinations of travel claims within a specific timeframe to ensure compliance.

Lack of an enforceable Conflict of Interest Policy. The organization should require everyone in the organization to sign and adhere to a Conflict of Interest Policy – especially anyone who handles money or has procurement authority.

Minimal internal controls and no segregation of duties. The organization does not have policies and procedures in place to establish controls on revenue and expenses. If an organization does not have adequate segregation of duties, an individual who prepares checks can cover his/her actions because the person also has access to the bank reconciliation statements.

The Organization's IT Systems Need Upgrading. The organization's databases and other software are not integrated or subject to adequate security measures. This scenario creates additional opportunities to manipulate data and records.

The bottom line is that fraud needs to be discussed openly in the organization. At the very minimum, the above issues should be addressed in the organization's Human Resources policies. If change is needed, then it must begin at the top. Do not expect the rest of the organization's employees to change their behavior unless they see that the board and senior management have adopted these measures as part of daily operations.

Talking Points in the Discussion about Fraud

The organization's senior management needs to lead the way in talking about fraud – and needs to be the visible source of policy-making in this area. When s/he talks about fraud, the discussion needs to be candid about the factors that support fraud and best practices that will be put into place to help the organization reduce the potential for fraud within its operations. It is equally important to emphasize that the Board and Chief Executive are committed to whistleblower protection and have instituted procedures to ensure that any type of retaliation is reported directly to senior management.

Don't be sidetracked by the long-time manager, or employee whose "feelings will be hurt" if protocols and expectations are changed. The well-being of your organization comes first. These individuals will just have to get over their "hurt" if they want to remain on the staff of the organization. If they don't get over their hurt, you have an obligation to the organization to move them out of the way so that genuine change can take hold.

Establishing A Safe and Effective System for Reporting Waste, Fraud and Abuse

Ongoing communication between management and employees is essential in ensuring that everyone understands why reporting waste, fraud and abuse is vital in keeping the organization safe and how investigations are conducted and findings presented. The organization's policies and procedures on whistleblower protection should contain the following features:

A confidential means for reporting suspected waste, fraud and abuse. Employees need to know how to go about filing the report and what types of evidence they should provide to substantiate their claims.

A process to thoroughly investigate any reports. Employees should also know how investigations are conducted and what will be expected of them in terms of providing a statement or answering questions.

A process for disseminating the findings from the investigation. The whistleblower should also know how the findings of the report will be disseminated.

No retribution for reports. The employee filing the complaint will not be subjected to termination, firing, harassment, or miss out on promotion. This is the most important part of the policy. All employees should know what their rights are under the Whistleblower Protection Policy.

Even if the findings do not support the essence of the complaint, the employee who made the complaint will not face any repercussions. Employees also need to understand that if they file a report in good faith and the findings don't support their claim, there will not be any repercussions.

Why Individuals Are Reluctant to "Blow the Whistle" On Waste, Fraud and Abuse

Everyone knows that whistle blowing is often viewed as a career limiting gesture, despite the fact that federal law prohibits retaliation. Whistleblowers are not universally embraced by management in any organization. Often they are described as "not a team player" or are categorized as troublemakers. Management can use tactics such as rumor and innuendo to make the whistleblower look bad.

Whistleblowers discover, despite the egregious financial irregularities that s/he has identified, that they have virtually no support from management. The situation is not remedied and wrongdoers are not held accountable. Negative responses to whistleblowers can be subtle, such as ostracism or moving the person's office to a less desirable location, but just as effective as explicit retaliation in silencing or discrediting the whistleblower. Other tactics include the silent treatment by supervisors or colleagues or even changing the location of the person's office or the type of equipment that is assigned to them. If this describes how whistleblowers are treated or viewed in your organization, you need to change the paradigm **NOW**.

Treating whistleblowers like snitches is like disabling your smoke detectors and fire alarms because you don't like the sound of the siren.

Senior management needs to send a clear message to all employees that reporting waste, fraud and abuse is crucial to the well-being of the organization and that there is a safe method to report any instance of retribution for reporting waste, fraud or abuse. Employees will not make these essential reports if they believe that it isn't safe and that there will be unpleasant consequences. Whether management approves or doesn't approve of the whistleblower's message is irrelevant. Federal law has instituted a Whistleblower Protection mechanism which is clear about prohibiting retribution of any kind – even the subtle acts. In today's legal environment management **can be held responsible** for "punishing" a whistleblower even in subtle ways. Having an effective Whistleblower Protection Policy is important not only because of the legal requirements, but to provide a mechanism which protects the organization's integrity and future viability.

Management needs to establish a system to protect whistleblowers, but also to encourage reporting of waste, fraud or abuse. The sooner that senior management knows about a potential problem, the sooner the problem can be handled. Consider Whistleblower Protection as an important factor in your organization's commitment to total quality management. Individuals who report problems with internal controls or procedures should be rewarded! They could very well have saved your organization time, money and labor. The report might also have identified a problem that, if ignored over time, could have resulted in a crisis.

Design of the Whistleblower Protection Policy

Every employee should have a copy of the whistleblower policy and it should be readily available for review in hard copy and online. This policy should also be covered in any orientation or training programs the business offers for its employees. The policy should clearly describe why whistleblower protection is necessary, how to file a report and the organization's commitment to protecting whistleblowers from retaliation.

Important! The organization's legal counsel should review the wording of the Whistleblower Protection Policy before it is released and provide advice whenever "whistleblower" reports are filed. The following sample policy includes "talking points" that should be included in an easy to understand policy.

Whistleblower protection policy checklist

Your organization needs to have:

- A Whistleblower Protection Policy
- A method for reporting waste, fraud or abuse
- Procedures for conducting investigations
- Protocols for disseminating findings (in conjunction with your legal counsel)

Whistleblower Protection Policy
[Note: The policy must be reviewed and approved by your organization's legal counsel. The talking points in this section are for informational purposes only.]

- The Whistleblower Protection Policy is being implemented at [your organization] to comply with federal law.

- At [your organization], any employee who reports waste, fraud or abuse will not be fired or otherwise retaliated against for making the report.

- The report will be investigated and even if determined not to be waste, fraud or abuse, the individual making the report will not be sanctioned. There will be no punishment including firing, demotion, suspension, harassment, failure to consider the employee for promotion, or any other kind of discrimination for reporting problems.

Methods for Reporting Waste, Fraud or Abuse

There are several ways in which your employees could report suspected waste, fraud or abuse.

- Contact the organization's ombudsman.

- Call the designated hotline that your organization has set up for this purpose.

- Send an email to a designated address that your organization has established for these types of reports.

- Make the report in writing.

Investigating the Report

Your organization should list the steps it would take to:

- Investigate the allegation

- Disseminate the report on our findings including providing the person filing a report with a summary of the findings.

- Take steps to deal with the issue addressed including making operational or personnel changes.

- If warranted, contact law enforcement to deal with any criminal activities.

The Role of Your Trusted Advisors in Preventing Fraud

Have one of your trusted advisors talk to employees about fraud. The perspective of professionals such as your insurance provider, banker or auditor will serve to reinforce the message that fraudulent activities inflict tremendous damage and that you mean business in taking action to combat fraud. These experts can offer suggestions to your employees about the important role they plan in deterring fraudulent activities in the organization as well as basic how to protect their personal finances from fraud.

Workplace Violence

On the day of the Virginia Tech shooting, one of my best clients asked me to come to his office. He is a senior executive in a large academic institution. He said, "Peg, what do you think?" I told him that he was the first client I ever had who wanted to discuss the topic! I also told him that his institution was a sitting duck (as was every other university in the U.S.). Workplace violence is one topic that triggers major denial. It won't ever happen here... Yes it can. Although Virginia Tech highlighted the risk areas in academic institutions, other examples in the business world are becoming more common. The disgruntled employee who was fired and comes back to his former workplace to wreak revenge on his superiors is now a more common scenario particularly in a difficult economy. Workplace violence is sometimes the spillover of domestic violence or an irate customer. In most cases, the violence begins without warning and there are often very few options for alerting the entire workplace or law enforcement before the person begins shooting.

Nature of the Organization's Business Operations

Whether an organization manufactures goods, provides services or acts as a distribution channel, the nature of its operations can present exposure to reputational risk. Companies that manufacture food, pharmaceuticals, chemicals, petroleum products or other items that are either perishable, fragile in terms of shelf life, or pose a potential safety risk can experience reputational crises when the products they manufacture are alleged to be defective in some way.

Organizations such as nonprofits or academic institutions experience reputational crises based on other types of events such as financial mismanagement, fraud or workplace violence. As your organization examines the potential for reputational crises within the institution, the nature of what it does to generate revenue needs to be scrutinized.

Some common problem areas include:

Nature of the operations including manufacturing and distribution of products that are either perishable or have a fragile shelf-life including pharmaceuticals, food and the like. Product safety is paramount to U.S. consumers and regulators. If the product you manufacture or sell is either unsafe or somehow compromised by unsafe ingredients/parts, the ensuing publicity and/or regulatory action can damage your organization's reputation.

Source of raw materials for the manufacturing process are not subject to rigorous quality assurance processes. The pet food contamination disaster in 2007 stemmed from the wheat gluten ingredient that was manufactured in China. The import firm generally engaged a quality assurance protocol, but seemingly did not in this instance. Other instances of lead-based paint being used on toys imported from China have also triggered consumer crises.

Warehousing of products or inventory can subject the products to hazards such as mold, water, excessive heat or cold, or other environmental hazards. If the organization's products are intended for human or animal consumption, it is important to carefully monitor the storage environment.

Production facilities. How many offices and/or manufacturing sites? The organization may have exposure due to the number and location of offices or factories. The greater the expanse of the organization, the more opportunity for communication and crisis missteps.

Product design. The design of a product(s) can establish a risk exposure for the organization, particularly if the product is alleged to cause harm to people, animals or the environment.

Transportation and Workplace safety. The quality and safety of the work environment of an organization can create an area of vulnerability if there have been accidents, injuries or negative attention from regulators such as OSHA. If the organization owns a fleet of cars or trucks, how are employees who drive for the organization screened? Do the vehicles require special licenses? Does the organization conduct random drug testing per US Department of Transportation requirements?

Employees who drive for the organization should be strictly prohibited from driving while using cell phones or text-messaging as is the law in several states. The signage on the organization's vehicles can create vulnerability if the employee is not driving in a safe manner, or is behaving in a way that does not bring credit to the organization.

Depending on the nature of the organization's products, the fleet of trucks or cars could also present the potential for hijacking, theft or other criminal activities either by employees or criminals.

Relations with the Community

Organizations need to live and work harmoniously in their communities. Today's business and community environments can also contain individuals or groups that have their own political agenda which may not include living harmoniously with your organization. Private sector firms such as Chiron and university researchers such as those at UCLA and UC Santa Cruz have been targets of animal rights and/or environmental activists who often break the law. These groups are some of the more extreme elements within a community, but honest, lower-key, non-violent political discord can also damage your organization's reputation.

Maintaining the organization's reputation as a good citizen can often center on simply maintaining good relationships with customers and the community at large. Strategies for effective public and media relations can be established in consultation with the organization's Public Relations advisor. This trusted advisor is essential in identifying those areas of your organization's relationship with the community that could trigger a reputational crisis.

Community relations checklist

- Location of your organization's offices, buildings, garages and/or manufacturing sites.

- Has your organization been the target of any community protests or complaints? If so, describe the nature of the complaints and/or protests.

- Actions that your organization's Public Relations department could recommend to improve the quality of the community relationships?

- Suggestions for the creation of a Community Relations Committee – task agenda and membership.

Some common problem areas include:

The organization does not handle complaints from customers and neighbors effectively. The way in which an organization treats customers and neighbors establishes its reputation in the community. If customers and neighbors know that the only way they can get the attention of the organization is to have the media investigate, then that's precisely what will happen whenever there is a complaint. If you recognize your organization in this statement, you need to take action now!

The organization does not cultivate good media relations. If your organization does not have an ongoing positive relationship with the local media outlets, then, in the event of an emergency or crisis, your designated spokesperson will not have the advantage of working with reporters and media outlets that are familiar with the organization. Your Public Relations trusted advisor can help you to establish this important set of relationships.

What are other issues that have either caused problems in the past or are causing problems now?

- Has the organization been targeted by community/environmental activists?
- Have these attacks created negative or adverse publicity?
- If this hasn't happened to your organization, has it happened to other companies in your industry?

Recognizing and identifying the issues behind community animosity is essential to doing what is necessary to maintain a positive reputation as an organization. Sometimes dealing with community issues takes the skill of a Public Relations expert. If your organization is having these problems without satisfactory resolution, your organization should add a Public Relations professional to your team of trusted advisors.

Technology and Cyber Risk

The nonprofit in this story is a household name because of its environmental work. Its website led the viewer through all the various programs and services that it had to offer. It even had a link for individuals to make donations. The development director and the technology director were shocked to discover that a porn site was soliciting donations for the nonprofit through a link in the porn site's web page. Viewers of the porn site were also directed to the environmental group's site. How did the environmentalists ever find out? The owners of the porn site proudly sent the environmental group a check for the donations that they had collected! The environmentalists' attorney sent the owners of the porn site a cease and desist letter and returned the check. This may be a very unusual example of how technology has the potential for damaging an organization's reputation, but it certainly points out how technology's reach is ever expanding.

Some common problem areas

In today's world of web-postings, blogs, Face Book pages and the like, your organization's brand and image can suffer even if the organization has not harmed anyone or has not produced defective products or has not damaged the environment.

Although an organization's reputation can be damaged by cyber risks, the unsupervised use of technology, particularly the internet, in the workplace can create a reputational crisis. For example, the *Washington Post* reported that the Inspector General found that the National Science Foundation had a severe problem with staff accessing porn on the agency's computers. One staff member claimed to watch porn 331 days of the previous year (O'Keefe, 2009).

Today's consumers also have web-based opportunities to express their displeasure for a company, nonprofit or university. Sometimes these reports are slanderous, but as was pointed out in Chapter 2, the senior management of Domino's Pizza had to deal with their reputational crisis by subscribing to a Tweet account for the purpose of combating the negative publicity generated by employees via u-Tube.

Your organization's website

Your organization's website is the electronic "face" of your organization. The way in which it is designed, its features (which make it user-friendly – or not) and the content say important things about your organization. Security is rapidly becoming one of the most significant challenges to websites – any website. All websites need to have firewalls and encryption software to protect client information and to ensure that transactions online with clients are secure. When a client puts a credit card number on your website, they and you need to feel confident that this sensitive information is properly encrypted and transported to the correct location. You should also consider including recommendations on your website for client safety in online transactions such as using a credit card, rather than a debit card, checking credit card statements to ensure that all the transactions are accurate, and, if possible, include a link to your local Better Business Bureau, Chamber of Commerce, or clearinghouse to verify that you are a member in good standing.

Who owns your website?

This question may seem counterintuitive but consider the case of the small nonprofit dance company. The organization had a volunteer who spent a significant amount of time working on projects. In fact this volunteer seemed to be everywhere at all times. The volunteer offered to design the dance organization's website and his efforts were lauded. One board member, however, found this individual's activities as well as his whole demeanor, suspicious. The board member went to the website www.whois.com and looked up the dance organization's website listing. Guess who owned the dance organization's website? That's right – the volunteer. Judging from his reaction when confronted, he never thought anyone from the board would ever think to check. The board had to request that the web company hosting the website take it down until the matter was settled. The nonprofit had to pay the volunteer sizeable sum to surrender the rights to the website.

Technology Policy

If your organization does not already have a technology policy, you need one now. All employees, from the CEO to the newest employee, must be required to read and sign your organization's technology policy. Your organization's technology policy should have these talking points:

- Clearly state that all of the organization's technology belongs to the organization. There are NO expectations of personal privacy when using the organization's technology. Employees need to understand that they may not use the organization's email for personal business or to send inappropriate messages to other staff, clients or anyone. All employees should also understand that the organization's internet access belongs to the organization. Web-surfing, access to porn sites or other inappropriate sites is strictly prohibited. Failure to comply should result in strict penalties including possible termination.

- Identify all of the organization's technology – hardware and software including laptop computers, desktop computers, hand-held devices such as PDAs and Blackberry, cell phones, internet access, email and all software programs purchased through the organization. Be aware that when electronic devices such as laptops or PDAs are "recycled" to another staff member, the "hard drive" of the device may still contain data, documents or transactions from the previous employee.

- Develop a policy on the storage and transportation of sensitive information out of your organization's facilities. Published reports describe multiple scenarios of laptops of bank employees being stolen that contained client financial data. The same thing could happen to your organization if you store sensitive information about clients, clients, or staff on laptops that leave your premises.

The policy should also have provisions on appropriate use of portable technology such as PDAs, cell phones, laptops. Safety and security issues need to be spelled out. In particular staff should be prohibited from discussing confidential information via cell phone and are prohibited from using the cell phone for personal business, or illegal uses such as crank calls or harassing another person. If your state prohibits the use of cell phones while driving, compliance with that law should be incorporated into the policy as well.

All employees who have access to any of the organization's technology should be required to read and sign the technology policy. Each person who signs the policy should have a copy of it to keep for his or her reference.

Technology policy checklist:

*   All aspects of the nonprofit's technology belongs to the organization. There are NO expectations of personal privacy when using the organization's technology.
*   Email and web access belong to the organization.
*   Examples of inappropriate email messages:

    Jokes

    Harassment

    Political commentary, particularly hate messages

    Anything you wouldn't want to read on the front page of your local newspaper, or have CNN broadcast.
*   The policy covers all of the organization's technology – hardware and software including laptop computers, desktop computers, hand-held devices such as PDAs and Blackberry, cell phones, internet access, email and all software programs purchased by the organization.
*   Requires returning of all electronic devices such as laptops or PDAs when leaving the employment of the organization.
*   Policy on the storage and transportation of sensitive information on laptops that leave your premises.
*   Staff who are entrusted with the organization's cell phones, laptops, PDAs or other electronics need to understand that they will be held personally accountable for the safety of the equipment, the safe use of the equipment, and the security of the data that is stored within these electronics.

Vendors and Outsourcing

All organizations deal with vendors for some form of product or service needed to operate. Outsourcing has become an efficient method of dealing with necessary functions that would be too costly to maintain in-house. The use of vendors and outsourcing has potential for creating reputational problems if employees engage in illegal or unethical transactions such as kick-backs or arranging to have the vendor or outsource organization provide the employee with products or funds.

Some common problem areas include:

Who in the organization deals with the vendors? How are vendors screened and supervised in terms of presenting the proper insurance coverage, invoicing, and provision of services per the terms of the contract. Just as financial operations duties should be segregated, procurement functions should also be segregated to ensure that vendor relationships are transparent.

Are any of the organization's functions outsourced? If so, how financially stable is the outsourcing vendor? If the organization outsources its payroll and/or HR functions, it is essential that the vendor is screened carefully to ensure financial stability and security measures are in place. Vendors should be required to provide proof of insurance. Call the vendor's insurance provider to verify coverage every year and/or policy period.

Checklist for vendors and outsourcing

- List the functions in your organization that are outsourced to vendors.
- Who in the organization deals with the vendors? List the employees and their supervisors. Identify the person responsible for verifying the vendor's insurance coverage.
- List the steps that are taken to segregate procurement functions within your organization.
- Vendors must provide: Appropriate insurance coverage and proof of insurance. Vendors must also provide contact information of his/her insurance provider so that the organization can verify that coverage is active. Verification of invoicing and provision of services per the terms of the contract. Your insurance professional should review the vendor's proof of insurance.

The Organization's Customer Service Model

As was noted in the Technology section, clients and customers readily access online evaluative sources such as Yelp, Facebook, or even email to express displeasure with a company, nonprofit or academic institution. As complaints about customer service in your organization increase, damage to your reputation worsens.

Some common problem areas include:

Your organization does not have a customer service process that addresses and resolves complaints. There is no mechanism to refer the complaint to a higher authority in the organization. Just as it is important to have a grievance process in place for employees, it is also vital to have a system in place to effectively deal with customer complaints. Customers who are frustrated in dealing with the organization will turn to other, more public, measures to voice their disapproval. Your organization needs to have a process to resolve customer complaints.

The number of complaints against your organization has resulted in a "failing grade" from the Better Business Bureau or has alerted state/federal regulators to investigate your organization. Your organization's reputation cannot afford to have a trusted third party, such as the Better Business Bureau issue this type of condemnation or have regulators or law enforcement begin to investigate.

Clients or customers have the opportunity to "rate" you on sites like Yelp. How can you neutralize a negative review or get it moved? Dissatisfied customers often turn to web-based resources to express their frustration. While they have the right to express an opinion, often the negative evaluations result in lost sales or overall decline in the organization's reputation.

Checklist for customer service:

Training

- Describe the type of customer service training that your employees receive.

- Are employees trained in techniques to "de-escalate" an agitated customer or client?

- Are employees trained in conflict resolution techniques?

- Are employees "empowered" to offer organizational resources to resolve a customer service issue? In other words, if resolving a customer complaint would require offering a refund or a discount on a future service, does the employee have the authority to offer these solutions?

Supervision

- Are supervisory personnel readily available to assist an employee in a customer service matter?

Incident history

- How often are customer service complaints lodged?

- Is there a pattern in terms of the specific complaints, i.e., defective products, customer does not feel that they received value for their money?

- In an nonprofit organization, do clients complain that the staff is rude, condescending or that the quality of the services are poor?

- Has the organization received negative ratings on a website such as Yelp?

Guilt by Association

What organizations do you have a formal relationship with such as a sponsor or strategic partnership?

Bank of America experienced a tidal wave of negative press since the Wall Street meltdown in the Fall of 2008. It, however, decided that continued association with ACORN, the ongoing nonprofit soap opera, was just too much to take. It's unlikely that Bank of America's association with this nonprofit would make much difference in terms of B of A's reputation, but its executives decided to distance themselves from the senior management of ACORN. There is a lesson in this scenario. When an associate organization is losing public trust, your organization must take steps to distance itself (Hagerty, 2009).

Some common problem areas to consider when associating with another organization include:

Before entering into a strategic relationship or a sponsorship, consider these potential reputational problems:

- Is the organization properly insured?
- Financial stability? Internal controls?
- Plan for dealing with crises?
- Nature of the associate's operations?
- Any previous reputational crises? If so, how were these resolved?

All of the questions listed above point to the quality of the organization's management and governance. Although the specific terms of the collaboration or sponsorship with the organization may appear to be neutral in terms of risk, it is important for your organization to ask the questions. The quality of the answers and the collaborator's willingness to provide the information will provide clues to the level of risk associated with relationship.

Next Steps

Examining Your Organization's Style and Culture

Could your organizational culture be fostering a reputational risk crisis?

Your organization's style and culture describes the intangible yet sometimes perceptible environment of the organization. The organizational culture encompasses how your organization's board and executives articulate the organization's values and principles. Maintaining the organization's good name and brand integrity is fundamental to its remaining a going concern. The issues raised in the areas of vulnerability outline those practices that have a high risk of triggering a reputational crisis. If your organization needs to change its business operations, it needs to begin by examining its organizational culture. The way that problems are described and solutions crafted is an integral part of the organization's culture.

Similarly, the culture sets the boundaries for rewards and punishment. Sometimes employees are told that management wants a particular type of behavior, but does nothing to reinforce the directive. Failure to reward desired behavior leads to extinguishing the very behavior that management encouraged! Conversely, undesirable behavior will be repeated if there are either no consequences or if the consequences are not timely, specific and unpleasant. Empty threats are as good as no consequences at all. When consequences for undesirable behavior are warned, managers and employees need to understand these consequences must be immediate and guaranteed.

The point of this discussion of organizational culture and ehavioral consequences is to candidly gauge how well employees in your organization would be expected to follow directives and adapt to new practices. If the answer is "not very well" then you will have to dramatically change the rewards and consequences – and be prepared to implement these quickly and in an unmistakable fashion. It is a new day in your organization, and you will need to send the message loud and clear that compliance with new policies and procedures is a condition of continued employment.

Identify Which of the Vulnerabilities Would Present the Most Immediate Problems

There are innumerable ways in which your organization could be damaged and/or the reputation of your organization tarnished. The point of this step is not to become bogged down in unending "what-if's" but to consider what the larger issues are in terms of managing risk within your organization. Consider the areas of vulnerabilities discussed in this chapter. Identify those areas that apply to your organization and begin to craft strategies to mitigate the risk.

Some ideas to begin the process:

• The Board and Senior Management must announce what changes that will be made in operational policies and procedures. If the impetus for change does not start at the top, no one will pay attention. New policies and practices need to be user-friendly. Employees need to understand what they are expected to do and NOT do. If your organization does nothing else, implementing an ironclad policy that requires employees to refer all media inquiries to the organization's designated spokesperson will serve to reduce the reputational risk of any crisis.

• Build the process to address what you are already doing (so you don't have to reinvent the wheel), and include those areas of improvement that you wanted to put into place. Don't engage in "paralysis by analysis" – keep it moving. Emphasize the processes that create efficiency, and ultimately, less work!

• Use the tools that you already have. Document the process using technology and ensure that copies of the new protocols and practices are widely disseminated. Also consider developing a one-page "shortcut" list to highlight what needs to be done to implement the new processes. The faster the employees can assimilate the desired behaviors into their daily routine, the faster the plan will solidify.

- Have your trusted advisors review the process once it is in place to ensure that it would make sense to a regulator or other stakeholder if necessary.

- This assessment of your organization's processes will be the foundation for the development of your Crisis Management Plan.

The Role of Your Trusted Advisors: Helping You to Mitigate Risk Areas in your Organization

Your organization's trusted advisors such as your insurance professional, your public relations advisor, your attorney and your financial advisor (banker or auditor) are important sources of advice and feedback. As you are working on developing the list of potential risk areas, discuss these findings with your trusted advisors. These individuals know your organization inside and out. They can identify areas that might not be on your list, or reassure you about some of the areas that you have listed.

Summary

The sources of reputational risk emerge from organizational dysfunction, poorly constructed internal controls and conditions that foster waste, fraud, abuse. Every organization has reputational vulnerabilities, but what is important is to recognize these vulnerabilities and take action to reduce the potential that these areas could contribute to a reputational crisis. Chapter 4 will present a streamlined Crisis Management Plan.

-four-

Crisis Management Plan
Dealing Effectively with an Emergency

*Once the indictment was handed down, clients started
jumping faster than they did off the Titanic.*

Arthur Bowman (Thomas & Fowler, 2002)

In Chapter 2 we saw that the Arthur Andersen accounting firm
imploded following the collapse of its major client, Enron, and its
indictment by the federal government. No one else wanted to be
associated with a firm so strongly linked to Enron's woes. Maybe
the executives at Arthur Andersen never even considered such a
scenario. Who knows if they even had a plan for dealing with a
reputational crisis this profound? If they had a plan, it certainly
was not executed very well.

To deal effectively with a reputational crisis, you will need a
plan – an effective crisis management plan [which will be referred
to as the "Plan"] that is customized for your organization and one
that contains a schedule for routine training and practice. In this
chapter we will examine the essential elements of a crisis management plan including strategies to ensure that everyone in the organization knows his/her role – and how to react to a crisis situation. Simply drafting a Plan does not ensure that everyone in the
organization will a) understand what they are expected to do, or b)
comply with these expectations. By incorporating the key elements
of the Plan into everyday work operations, your organization will

75

be better positioned to launch into action in the event of a crisis scenario.

Overview of a Generic Crisis Management Plan

The purpose of the Plan is to provide a framework for the organization's overall crisis management response. Preserving the organization's good name and image is inextricably linked to the quality of its response in an emergency or crisis situation. The focus of any crisis management plan is making the best possible use of available resources to cope with extreme conditions that endanger lives and property. Resources include personnel, materials, sites or facilities, and plans – intended methods and modes of action.

The organization's overarching goal in dealing with crisis situations is to ensure that the response to and recovery from a crisis takes place smoothly and efficiently. The organization should actively prepare in advance for emergencies by developing crisis response and recovery plans to ensure that the following objectives are met:

Protect life and ensure everyone's safety. One of the most damaging assertions in the wake of an emergency or crisis is that the organization's management did not take the necessary steps to save lives and avoid injuries. Preserving life and ensuring everyone's safety needs to be the top priority in any Plan.

Secure critical infrastructure and facilities including critical functions such as IT and manufacturing. The Plan needs to be clear about taking the steps necessary to secure the organizational infrastructure, particularly IT and those organizational departments critical to resumption of normal operations.

Support the resumption of normal business operations. The Plan needs to contain measures that will promote a rapid move from crisis scenario to the resumption of normal operations. Everyone in your organization must understand their role in resumption of operations.

Generic Crisis Management Plan

Plan Component	What it looks like in action
Declaring an emergency: • Launch the Crisis Management Plan • Evacuation or Shelter in Place announcements • Launching the Crisis Communication Plan	1. Alerting management; employees of the crisis – and possibly action such as evacuation or shelter in place 2. Media communications – can be a prepared statement 3. Stakeholder communications – can initially be a prepared statement
Dealing with the crisis: Action steps and ongoing communication	Specific actions taken to resolve/ mitigate the crisis. This component may take hours, days or weeks depending on the nature of the crisis.
Move toward Resumption of Normal Operations	Steps needed to begin the process of resuming normal operations
Post-crisis debrief	Determining the source of the crisis; how to reduce the potential for a future event of that nature; What can be learned from the event and response.
Adjustments Make Necessary Changes in the Organization and How it Operates	Take steps to modify the source of the crisis including HR action and operational action.

Structure of the Plan

Assumptions. The Plan is built with certain assumptions in mind. The first assumption is that the individuals directing the crisis response have been chosen and trained in advance. Examples of individuals whose C-level positions in the organization are consistent with crisis management skills include:

- Chief Executive of the organization
- Chief Operations Officer
- Chief Financial Officer
- Chief of Security
- Chief Information Officer

The second assumption is that your organization's Plan includes contingencies to address those crises that could be triggered by the vulnerabilities that you identified for your organization from the discussion in Chapter 3. Although no one can ever predict the exact nature or "flavor" of a crisis scenario, the risk profile of your organization should give you an idea of the types of scenarios that would be more likely for your geographic region and nature of operations.

The third assumption is that the structure of the Plan you prepare for your organization clearly reflects its structure and focus as well as that of the geographic region(s) in which your organization's buildings/offices are located. For example, a crisis management plan for a firm that manufactures food products in multiple locations throughout the United States will look very different from a crisis management plan designed for a nonprofit located in a small town in the Midwest, a retail establishment in San Francisco or a university in New England.

Lastly, the structure of the Plan assumes that the impetus for the design and execution of the Plan comes directly from the organization's Chief Executive and Board. Without explicit direction from the Executive leadership to build the Plan, assign crisis management roles in advance and implement an ongoing training agenda, the organization is wasting its time.

Plan Components

The crisis management plan is designed to outline a sequence of activities that will facilitate an effective response to an emergency or crisis situation. Keep in mind that the specific nature of a crisis need not be something spectacular such as an earthquake, tornado or fire. A crisis situation involving fraud, financial mismanagement, product contamination or technology does not necessary present physical danger or damage to property, but does need a coherent, effective response. Each of the Plan components provides a set of directions to those in crisis response leadership.

The crisis management plan configuration shown in the chart is deliberately generic to allow you to create a customized Plan for your organization. Regardless of how your organization is structured, the crisis management plan you create will need to have each of these Plan components in some form.

Declaring an Emergency

Plan Component	What It Looks Like In Action

Declaring an emergency:
 	
• Launch the Crisis Management Plan
 	
• Evacuation or Shelter in Place announcements
 	
• Launch the Crisis Communication Plan
	1. Organization's Chief Executive launches the Crisis Management Plan
	
	   • Alerting the organization of the emergency or crisis.
	
	   • If applicable – broadcast evacuation or shelter in place orders.
	
	2. Media communications – can be a prepared statement.
	
	3. Stakeholder communications – can initially be via prepared statements.

Launch the Crisis Management Plan

The crisis management plan cannot be launched until an emergency is declared. As soon as anyone in the organization becomes aware of a real or potential crisis, s/he must be required to alert their immediate supervisor, and if the situation warrants, to call 911. *The supervisor must, in turn, be required to alert a member of Executive Management.* Time is of the essence. If your organization does not have these rules in place, you could lose valuable time in launching the Plan and the subsequent delay could damage the organization's reputation.

Following a declared state of emergency the organization's Chief Executive or designee must alert the Designated Spokesperson. The Designated Spokesperson will provide information to the media if instructed to do so by the organization's Chief Executive or Crisis Management Leader. Appropriate information must be provided routinely to employees to enable their cooperation in a potential crisis. Employees will be reminded that all media inquiries must be directed to the Designated Spokesperson at a specified telephone number.

Authority

The organization's executives will direct the overall response to the crisis. The Designated Spokesperson, under the direction of the organization's Chief Executive, will have the authority to disseminate information to the media and the public. Except for emergency services personnel such as firefighters and police officers, only the Designated Spokesperson should be authorized to provide information to the media. Once a crisis/emergency has been identified, the organization's security staff will have the authority to limit access to the affected area and any other areas of organization's property designated for use in responding to the crisis.

Immediate Responses: Evacuation and Shelter in Place Protocols

The crisis management plan needs to be very clear about protocols for evacuation and shelter-in-place protocols including what signals will be sounded to identify each of the responses as well as a third signal to represent "all clear." The protocols presented in this chapter are intended to be samples for your consideration as you prepare your organization's crisis management plan.

Evacuation Protocols

Be sure that the Plan includes specific information about:

- Location of nearest emergency exits, fire extinguishers and fire alarm pull stations.

- Description of the evacuation routes, and assembly areas for your work site and building.

- Evacuation Meeting Locations are places for your department/ unit staff to gather and wait for instructions and/or the "all clear" notification by emergency response personnel. Be sure to also include the location of alternate meeting locations

- Evacuation meeting locations should be easily and safely accessible.

- Large departments with staff in more than one building will have more than one evacuation meeting location.

- For building evacuations (fire alarms), NEVER assemble in any building where the fire alarm is sounding. Continue to move to a safe area.

- For large-scale emergency evacuations (fire, tornado or earth-quake), building employees should proceed to the designated evacuation meeting locations, when instructed by emergency services personnel. In the event of a tornado, employees should move to the designated Tornado Shelter area in the building.

Everyone in the organization needs to understand what actions they must take if the signal for evacuation is given or if the signal for "shelter in place" is given. Here are some examples of each type of protocol.

Example of an Evacuation Protocol

Evacuation procedures:

1. Identify stairways, doors or other emergency exits [Your organization should have floor Plans posted in strategic places in your offices. The floor plans should clearly identify the closest exits.]

2. Location where all employees, clients, visitors are to meet so that management team can do a headcount [Identify a Primary meeting place and an Alternate meeting place for your organization's employees.]

3. Protocols to assist police, firefighters and other emergency personnel

In the event of a fire

Evacuate the building and relocate through stairwells not elevators to the ground floor. If your building has an intercom system to announce emergencies, be sure that the emergency announcement can be heard on all floors and in all offices.

- Alert all persons and ask them to remain calm but move quickly. In an emergency scenario, every moment counts. The calmer that the employees and visitors remain, the faster they can evacuate the building.

- Listen for instructions and report to the designated emergency exits. Employees should be trained ahead of any crisis situation to listen for instructions and know where the nearest emergency exit is. Once out of the buildings, employees should know that they are prohibited from returning to the building until the "all clear" signal is given.

- Emergency meeting place – There should actually be two emergency meeting places. If, for some reason, it is not safe to congregate at the primary meeting place, employees need to know where the alternative meeting place is. As part of the disaster drills, employees should occasionally be directed to meet at the alternative meeting place.

- Everybody has to be accounted for before any member of employees, visitors and others are permitted to leave the premises. It is important that the Designated Spokesperson have a list of individuals who have been accounted for, a list of individuals who were not in the building that day and a list of individuals who have not been accounted for. This list should be given to the fire captain so that emergency responders will have an idea of how many people may still be in the building. *Employees should understand that full cooperation in terms of census-taking is mandatory and that failure to cooperate may result in disciplinary action.*

- Keep clear of the building to avoid falling debris. Once employees have assembled and are accounted for, it is important that they understand to keep a safe distance from the building and stay out of the way of emergency responders.

Example of a Shelter-in-Place Protocol

In the event of workplace violence

When the signal to shelter in place is given, all employees, clients and visitors must take shelter in the nearest office or room with a door.

- The people in the room need to seek shelter in a corner or area to the left or right of the door if possible. Do NOT gather near the door or directly across from the door.

- Push a piece of furniture up against the door or take some other measure to secure the door from being pushed in from the outside.

- Depending on the workplace violence situation that triggered the order it may be necessary to maintain silence.

- If possible, use a cell phone to text message the organization's security team or 911 to advise that X number of people are located in _____room in _____building.
- Remain in the room until the all-clear signal is given.

In the event of a tornado or severe storm

Although tornados tend to occur in specific areas of the country, changing weather patterns make for an increase in the incidents of tornados and severe thunder storms throughout the country. Tornados are associated with thunderstorms, but not all thunderstorms contain tornados. Severe thunderstorms, however, have been known to contain damaging winds, severe lightning and hail. Employees, clients and visitors should be warned about this type of weather and be given shelter for the duration of the storm.

If the building has a basement, the staff, clients and visitors should be directed to the basement of the buildings. Otherwise, the bathrooms and stairways of the building will provide the best protection during a tornado. The crisis management plan should indicate which buildings have basements and which have other architectural features that could house people in the event of a tornado or severe storm.

If your area is affected by tornados and/or severe thunder storms, the Plan should include an instruction such as:

> *If you hear a siren and/or tornado advisory announcement, please proceed to one of those areas and follow the procedures outlined below.*

When a tornado *warning* is issued, it means that a tornado has actually been sighted or has been indicated by radar, and that this or other tornadoes may strike in your vicinity. Public warning will come over the radio, TV, or by [give the warning signals used for tornadoes in your area if applicable.] **Take the following actions immediately!**

Shelter-in-Designated Area

Your Plan needs to specify how an announcement about a tornado or severe storm will be made [public address system, text message, email, computer screen warning]- to warn employees that a tornado warning has been issued for your area and that it is advisable to have all employees move to a safe location in the building. Take the following actions immediately:

- Get away from the perimeter of the building and exterior glass. If time permits, close drapes, blinds, etc.

- Leave your office if it is located on the building's perimeter - close the door.

- Go to the center of the building - bathrooms or stair enclosures. Sit down and protect yourself by putting your head as close to your lap as possible, or you may kneel while protecting your head.

- Do not use elevators and do not go to the lobby or outside the building.

- Keep your radio or television set tuned to a local station for information.

- Do not use the telephone to get information or advice. This only ties up circuits. Updated information will be passed on to you via the [specify the means] as often as possible.

In Chapter 5 we will examine the way in which the Plan would work in a number of scenarios. It is important to consider the types of emergency scenarios relevant to your organization that would call for either evacuation or shelter in place protocols. Be realistic –if your location is not seismically active, don't worry about earthquakes. If your organization is in the mountains, your chances of being affected by a tornado are very low. Develop generic plans for those types of scenarios that are likely to happen.

Launch the Crisis Communication Plan

The Crisis Communication Plan is launched as soon as the first announcement is made of the emergency. The purpose of the Crisis Communication Plan is to advise the organization's internal community and external stakeholders including the public about important issues and developments. The crisis communication plan should include a variety of approaches to ensure that emergency communications are received by employees and other stakeholders in the event that one of the means of communications is either blocked on temporarily disabled. The identity and contact information for the organization's Designated Spokesperson should be widely disseminated throughout the organization. Having a policy to refer all media inquiries to the Designated Spokesperson will not be successful if employees do not know who the Designated Spokesperson is or how to reach the individual. There should also be at least two back-up spokespersons. They should have the same contact information (organization cell phone number) and everyone in the organization should know who they are as well. When the emergency is announced, the identity of the designated spokesperson should be given at the same time if possible.

Initial Crisis Communication – Alerting the organization to the emergency

Once the crisis management plan has been launched by the organization's Chief Executive, employees, clients and visitors need to be advised that an emergency is declared. This can be achieved via:

- Alarms and/or sirens to direct people to evacuate or shelter in place.
- Text messages.
- Email or IT system that broadcasts a message onto the screens of all computers in use.
- A phone tree is a structured plan that features specific calling patterns for identified leaders. Once the emergency has been declared executives and managers put the phone tree into play. Everyone who has obligations to make phone calls knows in

advance who s/he is to call. The phone tree needs to have contact information that is up to date and also should have alternative phone numbers for each person. The alternative phone numbers could also include family members' contact information. For example, Mary Smith's home phone and cell phone could be listed, but her husband's cell phone could be listed as an alternative number. The organization needs to assure staff that the alternative numbers will never be used unless: 1) there is an emergency and, 2) the primary numbers were not successful in reaching the staff member.

- The organization's website can be a source for information and also a conduit to accept emergency donations. The web address can be included in press releases so that the public can contact the organization.

The phone tree should include multiples contact methods:

- phone(s) – office contact number and alternate number such as cell phone
- text message,
- pager

Identify primary and secondary sources of information – and phone numbers including cell phone numbers/personal email addresses. Secondary contact information to be used only in an emergency.

Include a plan to communicate emergency notifications and instructions to your employees during regular and non-working hours. Suggestions:

- Managers must identify key department individuals *in advance or an emergency*, who will function as emergency information contacts and coordinators to receive and distribute information to employees.
- Establish a Department "Telephone Tree" and Hotline (voice mailbox) to provide information updates and instructions.
- Departments should maintain up-to-date employee contact

liststo ensure that employees can be contacted in case of an emergency (if key personnel need to be called back to campus, or be consulted for crucial decisions and information, e.g. fire, chemical spill or a crime over a weekend).

- Update your phone tree at least twice a year and send updated copies to the organization's Crisis Management Team.

Communication and Media Relations Plan

The Designated Spokesperson

The crisis communication plan needs to have a designated spokesperson and at least two back-up spokespeople. The names and contact information for these people should be common knowledge to everyone in the organization. The Designated Spokesperson must take steps to ensure the quality and suitability of all communication materials. As part of the planning process, the Designated Spokesperson activities should be outlined. For example, the Designated Spokesperson would be responsible for meeting initially and maintaining contact with the executive management to determine level of crisis and constituencies affected. Once initial information on the emergency/crisis has been verified, the designated spokesperson arranges for the information and updates to be prepared for employees, customers and other stakeholders. The designated spokesperson is also responsible for coordinating with the organization's IT or web design departments to ensure that information on the emergency/crisis is posted on the organization's website of provided via a telephone recording.

Preparing and dissemination information for external audiences including the media is one of the most important tasks for a designated spokesperson. As part of this role, the spokesperson may be expected to establish a media center either on or off the organization's property, establish and maintain Hot Lines for the public, clients and customers during and after a crisis as appropriate. Some of the more challenging aspects of the designated spokesperson's role include responding to media inquiries regarding the crisis and managing the media's presence during the crisis.

To ensure that the appropriate information is disseminated and reported the designated spokesperson needs to monitor media coverage and public response to the crisis. Throughout the crisis, the quality of the communications process needs to be constantly assessed and reported on to the Chief Executive and the Executive Team.

Employees must understand that they have an obligation to refer all media inquiries to the Designated Spokesperson and that there will be swift and unpleasant consequences for failure to abide by this rule. The intent of such a policy is to safeguard the image of the organization by ensuring that only appropriate and accurate information is disseminated. In the midst of a crisis some information is not yet available or in the process of being determined. The Designated Spokesperson can ensure that developing information is disseminated in a timely fashion.

Prepared statements are an efficient way to make certain that a press release contains all of the necessary information on the status of the crisis. Drafting prepared statements as part of the planning process means that the organization's spokesperson can simply fill in the blanks to provide the media with an articulate statement describing the situation and providing the relevant information. Because your organization's image is directly correlated to the credibility and professionalism displayed during a crisis, consider using the planning process to also arrange for media training and coaching in drafting of prepared statements for the organization's designated spokespersons.

A prepared statement that can be used in the event of a crisis – the statement is prepared in advance and has these talking points:

- Give basic facts – name of the organizations, location and brief description of the organization's mission.
- The statement should have a section (that would be filled in when a crisis occurs) that describes (there should not be any detail until facts and circumstances can be verified):
- What happened in very general terms
- Who was involved
- When the crisis occurred

- Where the crisis occurred
- Information on how to contact the organizations
- The organization's commitment to the community and its customers

The prepared statement should also have information tailored to the needs of employees, customers and other stakeholders.

- In the event of a crisis, employees need to know how to obtain information on the situation and what is expected of them in terms of service.
- Clients will need to know how to contact the organizations to either obtain goods and services or how they might contact alternative resources.

Media Relations

Cultivating good media relations is essential for all organizations in good times as well as in a crisis situation. The investment of time and energy needed to establish good relations with the media will pay dividends when a crisis hits. The organization's Designated Spokesperson should ensure that the media contacts have up to date contact information and the names of the back-up designated spokespersons. The Designated Spokespersons are the "go to" individuals who can provide the media with the most accurate information at any given moment in time. It is worth the time and energy to ensure that the organization's media contacts have the full contact information for the Designated Spokespersons as this will increase the probability that the media calls them first.

Media Contacts

The crisis management plan should contain a section in which your organization can list important media contacts. The Plan presumes that the Designated Spokesperson is trained to handle media inquiries and how to establish a productive relationship with the media in advance of a crisis incident. Having a clear set of procedures for crisis communications is important.

Disseminating Crisis Information to Stakeholder Groups

The Designated Spokesperson's primary focus is ensuring that accurate and useful information is disseminated to employees, stockholders, customers, other stakeholders and the public at large. Information needs to be tailored to meet the needs of the specific constituency group. For example, employees need to know where to report to work and when. Stockholders probably only care that there is a company still in place. Customers want to know if and when their order will be delivered. The media will want to know about the details of the crisis. As part of your organization's planning, you should identify the topic areas relevant to each of your stakeholder groups would want to be included in.

Employees Employees will need to know about an array of topics. The organization will need to determine the extent to which employees are briefed on the nature of the crisis. Privacy and legal issues might need to be taken into consideration depending on the nature of the crisis. Your organization's trusted advisors such as attorneys, public relations advisor and insurance professional should be consulted. If the crisis involved an incident such as a fire, employees will need logistical information such as where to report to work, work hours and other operational information.

Clients, customers and students Information that should be conveyed to these important stakeholders on where to obtain services, information on the extent to which the organization's current programmatic offerings are impacted by the crisis and where to call to obtain information.

Vendors Vendors need to know where the organization is operating and how to get in touch with the individual(s) handling vendor inquiries.

Financial institutions Banks, stock brokerages and other financial institutions will want to know where the organization is currently conducting business, names of individuals who are authorized to transact business and if any board protocols on emergency financial operations have been triggered. Remember, the financial institutions will want to see documents and have documentation in place (such as signatures) prior to the crisis incident for any individuals who would be authorized to transact business. Remember, the bank or other financial institutions are limited by the organizations written instructions in who is authorized to do business with the bank to protect the interests of the organization.

Public Public inquiries need to be addressed by means of a general statement providing information on how to contact the organization, the contact information for the spokespersons or their designees, and information on how to make a donation to the organization.

Dealing with the crisis

Plan Component	What it looks like in action
Dealing with the crisis: Action steps and ongoing communication	Specific actions taken to resolve/mitigate the crisis. This component may take hours, days or weeks depending on the nature of the crisis.

The Plan should describe a set of generic action steps to provide a framework for response to crisis situations that could impact normal operations. The primary goal of these actions is to provide a coordinated response that protects life, property, and the organization's good name. Chapter 5 elaborates on the action steps that need to be taken in specific emergency situations. The Plan needs to present generic actions that are part of any emergency response.

Response to the immediate crisis The Plan should be clear about the primary requirement to listen and follow instructions. The crisis scenario that your organization experiences may be different from a fire, earthquake or tornado event. While everyone in the organization needs to understand the appropriate response to a variety of crises scenarios, the most important response is to do what they are told to do – particularly if firefighters, EMT personnel or police officers are on the scene. These First Responders are trained to take control of the situation. Employees need to know that during an emergency it is essential that they cooperate fully with all instructions.

Context of the Plan

The Plan should establish who is in charge as well as the crisis management structure within your organization. The Plan needs to identify who is in charge in the event that an emergency or crisis is declared. There need to be at least two other individuals designated as back-up leaders. The designated leader and the back-ups need to assemble a Crisis Management Team composed of key individuals within the organization and at least one back-up for each member of the team. The Crisis Management Team will be the group responsible for launching the Crisis Management Plan.

A generic structure for the management of emergencies. Crisis and emergencies play out in very different ways. Having a generic crisis management plan in place will facilitate the design of a crisis management plan that suits the needs and structure of your organization. As your organization prepares its Plan, consider the areas of vulnerabilities present within your organization. Designing a Plan with these vulnerable areas in mind will help the organization to focus on the essential action steps.

Develop a training agenda for employees on the basics of crisis preparedness and response as these play out in various scenarios. The relevant details of the Plan need to be shared across the organization. In Chapters 5 and 6 we will examine how the Plan addresses various crisis situations and the ways in which your organization should offer preparedness training to all employees.

Establish clear channels of communication. Clear, concise and honest communication is the foundation for effective response to any crisis. The organization's crisis communication element within the Plan establishes communication channels internal to the organization and external to the organization's important stakeholders including the public. The Plan is designed to facilitate communication and decision making during emergencies in a strategic manner that will ensure coordination of information and resources among local and regional First Responder agencies.

- Key Staff must keep a copy of the Plan on a portable device -- Be sure that all key people have a copy of the Plan in soft copy (preferably on their PDA or Blackberry) or a paper copy.

- The Organization will establish web access/easy access to staff availability checklists. Management needs to be able to see all of the completed Staff Availability worksheets.

The Plan should include a means by which supervisors can determine if employees are able to return to work and/or their availability for work shifts other than their normal work hours.

Employee availability checklist

- Employee Name
- Department
- Active Phone Number
- Present Residence Address
- Home E-mail
- Any injuries to employee?
- If yes, nature of injury
- Any injuries to family member?
- If yes, nature of injury
- Any serious damage to employee member's property?
- Best times for this employee person to work his or her shift

- Any time this employee person could not work? Why? Transportation: Does this person have transportation?
- Can this person assist others in getting to work?

The Plan is primarily an administrative guide for rapid communication and decision-making as it outlines the functions, duties and responsibilities necessary for the effective response to crisis situations.

After the Crisis is Over

Movement toward Normal Operations. Once the crisis has been resolved, the organization enters a recovery phase that moves the company, nonprofit or academic institution from the crisis mode toward resumption of business operations. The crisis management plan needs to provide guidance and direction toward the organization's larger business resumption plan. Information on Business Resumption Planning, or Business Resiliency, can be found in the Resources section of this book.

After the crisis

Plan Component	What it looks like in action
Move toward Resumption of Normal Operations	Identify steps needed to begin the process of resuming normal operations
Post-crisis debrief	Determining the source of the crisis; how to reduce the potential for a future event of that nature; What can be learned from the event and response.
Adjustments Make Necessary Changes in the Organization and How it Operates	Take steps to modify the source of the crisis including HR action and operational action.

Post-Crisis Debrief

The Post-Crisis debrief can take place within days of the crisis, or several weeks after launching the crisis management plan. Determining factors on the timing of the debrief include the specific nature of the crisis, how long it is taking to resume normal operations and the overall quality of the resiliency of the operations. The debrief should center on:

- **Determining the source of the crisis.** Once the source of the crisis is ascertained, the Crisis Management Team in conjunction with the Board and Chief Executive can move to mitigate the circumstances contributing to the crisis, or modify the organizational structure to dramatically limit the potential for reoccurrence.

- **What can be learned from the event and response?** The Chinese character for "crisis" also represents the character for "opportunity." No matter how devastating the crisis was, the event still holds great opportunity for learning and for organizational change. The response should be critiqued to determine if another response model might render better results. The crisis management and crisis communication responses need to be critiqued to determine how effective these were in managing the crisis itself and in communicating with internal and external stakeholders.

Summary

The generic Plan presented in the chapter addresses the primary phases of a crisis scenario. The Plan needs to be representative of the organization's unique features and communication needs. In Chapter 5, the Plan will be shown as it might function in various crisis scenarios.

five

Action!
Launching the Crisis Management Plan

The tragedy of September 11th provided many important lessons about crisis management planning. Morgan Stanley was one of the companies that had offices in the World Trade Center. This company was well-aware of the damage that a terrorist attack could produce. In 1993 terrorists bombed the World Trade Center inflicting heavy damage on the Morgan Stanley offices. Morgan Stanley's management understood that the terrorists were persistent in their mission and another attack was inevitable. Following the 1993 bombing, Morgan Stanley brought in a consultant to engage in monthly disaster drills. The operative instruction was that during one of these drills, everyone was to exit the building via the nearest emergency exit. No exceptions. No excuses. These drills took place every month for the next eight years. On September 11th when the alarm sounded, everyone in the Morgan Stanley offices evacuated the building and kept moving. Although any loss of life is tragic, only six (6) members of the Morgan Stanley staff lost their lives that morning.

The World Trade Center also housed nonprofit organizations as well as corporations. British royal, Sarah Ferguson, Duchess of York, had an office in the World Trade Center for her foundation, Chances for Children. In an interview after the September 11th attacks, CNN's Larry King asked the Duchess how long she anticipated it would take for her foundation to resume operations and if she was planning to reopen her foundation offices in another location. The Duchess replied," Larry, the foundation is already up and running. We raised close to $100,000 for the 9/11 Fund which we started... Chances for Children is up and running..." (Transcript, Larry King Live, CNN, November 16, 2001).

The two important lessons from these examples are:

1. **Crises are a part of the life of any organization and should be expected to occur.** Taking action to preserve life and safety should be every organization's number one priority. Having a plan in place to help keep people safe is essential, but only consistent and ongoing practice will make the plan work effectively. All disasters, emergencies and crises have reputational implications particularly if people are injured or killed because the organization did not have measures in place to help people survive the incident.

2. **Crises, even ones as catastrophic as the events of September 11th, need not destroy the business, nonprofit or academic institution** if a plan is in place to manage the crisis incidents and resume business operations.

This chapter will present ideas and recommendations for the design of an action strategy for your organization's crisis management plan based on the Plan designed in Chapter 4. How your organization handles the crisis does have implications for your organization's brand and image. Just as Chapter 2 provided some illustrations what you should not do in handling a crisis, this chapter will guide you through the important steps of effectively implementing a crisis management plan. As your organization designs its Plan, be aware that the Plan will play out differently depending on the nature of the crisis scenario. The Plan and everyone in the organization need to be flexible in crafting an apporpriate response.

Who's in Charge? Crisis Incident Management Leadership

Everyone in your organization must be aware of who is in charge in an emergency or crisis. This leadership assignment needs to have at least one back-up identified for each of the key roles. The CEO or Executive Director may seem to be a logical choice, but in an emergency, this individual could either be out of town, or tasked with other emergency-related obligations. The crisis management plan should identify those individuals – and back-ups that will coordinate the organization's crisis response and subsequent business resumption.

Some key roles in activating the crisis management plan include:

Chief Executive of the organization This individual or his/her designee triggers the crisis management plan by declaring an emergency.

Crisis Management Team These individuals have been designated by the leader of the organization to coordinate the crisis response. The team that is working directly to create the organization's crisis management plan is the primary liaison between the planning process and the activation of the Plan. The Crisis Management Team can include key managers within the organization as well as leaders of critical divisions such as IT, Finance and Manufacturing.

Designated Spokesperson This individual and his/her back-ups are key to ensuring that timely, accurate information is provided to internal and external stakeholders including the media.

Trusted Advisors These individuals, particularly the organization's insurance professional and public relations professional, have critical roles in assisting the organization in responding to the crisis.

Board of Directors The organization's board leadership in managing the crisis scenario is also crucial. The board needs to prepare for a crisis in advance by fully participating in crisis management planning, and preparing documents, such as emergency protocols for financial management, that can be triggered in the event of an emergency.

The Organization's Expectations of Employees

Your organization needs to be clear about what it expects from employees in the event of a crisis or emergency. Staff may be called upon to work hours that are different from their normal work times, or work in shifts. A nonprofit may ask its volunteers to report at a specific location to help with additional tasks. Although staff may be advised that new work expectations and hours are conditions of their employment, volunteers are under no obligation to undertake additional tasks.

Other expectations would include employee cooperation in directing all media inquiries to the organization's Designated Spokesperson. The organization needs to be very clear about how to reach the Designated Spokesperson and that information should be readily available to all staff. Employees also need to fully understand the rationale for this policy and the consequences for noncompliance. The policy should be shared with employees as a normal part of their orientation curriculum and in routine in-service sessions which review the procedures and expectations in the event of an emergency.

Employees could also be involved in other divisions within the company, nonprofit or academic institution. For example, employees could be instructed to assist in emergency customer service and order fulfillment. Employees that are transferred to an area outside of their normal working assignment need to be carefully screened in advance. Before employees begin their assignments, they need to be briefed on the scope of their work, the potential impact that their words, actions and behavior could have on the organization's good name, and what is expected in terms of schedule and productivity.

Examples of Emergency Situations

As your organization considers how to activate the crisis management plan, an important element to consider is the type(s) of logistics that would be necessary to execute the Plan. This section of the Plan provides recommendations for setting up action steps to execute the crisis management plan in various crisis scenarios.

Emergency Situations Requiring Evacuation

Your crisis management plan should include specific instructions on evacuation procedures. These instructions might vary if your organization has multiple buildings and/or multiple sites. Everyone, however, needs to understand how to safely evacuate from the building in which they are located.

Emergency	Initial Action	Follow-up
Fire	• Alert main desk to call 911. • Remain calm • Note your location using evacuation map. • Move in an orderly fashion toward the stairs, exit the building. • Close all doors as you exit. • Don't use elevators. • Once outside, move away from the building.	• Headcount at gathering site. • Report names of individuals not accounted for to firefighting authorities.

Emergency	Initial Action	Follow-up
Earthquake	• Stay calm • "Duck and Cover" • Stay clear of tall objects and windows. • Stay under cover until the initial shocks have subsided	• Meet in the designated area. • Ensure that staff, clients and others in the office are accounted for. • Advise emergency personnel if anyone is missing.

Your Plan should include this information to successfully execute an evacuation of the building:

- **Location of stairways, doors or other emergency exits.** Employees should be trained ahead of any crisis situation to listen for instructions and know where the nearest emergency exit is. Once out of the buildings, employees should know that they are prohibited from returning to the building until the "all clear" signal is given.

- **Alert all persons and ask them to remain calm but move quickly.** In an emergency scenario, every moment counts. The calmer that the employees and visitors remain, the faster they can evacuate the building. Be sure that your Plan includes contingencies for the evacuation of staff/visitors that are sight-impaired, mobility-impaired or hearing-impaired.

- **Location where all employees, clients, visitors are to meet so that management team can do a headcount [Identify a Primary meeting place and an Alternate meeting place for Your Organization's employees].** There should actually be two emergency meeting places. If, for some reason, it is not safe to congregate at the primary meeting place, employees need to know where the alternative meeting place is. As part of the disaster drills, employees should occasionally be directed to meet at the alternative meeting place.

- **Head Count.** Everybody has to be accounted for before any member of employees, visitors, etc. are permitted to leave the premises. It is important that the crisis management team have a list of individuals who have been accounted for, a list of individuals who were not in the building that day, and a list of individuals who have not been accounted for. This list should be given to the fire captain so that emergency responders will have an idea of how many people may still be in the building. Employees should understand that full cooperation in terms of census-taking is mandatory and that failure to cooperate may result in disciplinary action.

Emergency Situations Requiring Shelter-In-Place

During a situation that requires employees to shelter in place, it is essential that systems be in place to notify everyone to begin the shelter-in-place action. The message can be given via an alarm signal, telephone recordings that are programmed to ring all phones and deliver the message, computer alerts which pop up on the screen or other means that would work for your organization. Speed and saturation are the key elements. Everyone on the premises needs to know to shelter in place NOW. The activation plan also needs to identify how the "all clear" signal will be given.

Emergency	Initial Action	Follow-up
Tornado	Get away from the outside walls of the building and exterior glass. If time permits, close drapes, blinds, etc. Go to the center of the building - bathrooms or stair enclosures. Sit down and protect yourself by putting your head as close to your lap as possible, or kneel while protecting your head.	Once the "all clear" signal has been sounded, meet in the designated area for a head-count. Alert First Responders to the location of individuals who were on premises, but are missing from head count.
Workplace violence	Alert the main desk or a supervisor. Take steps to shelter in place.	Report suspicious activity immediately. Take threats of violence seriously and report these to management.

Emergency Situations Requiring Special Communication and Action

Some situations, such as product contamination, require immediate action and special communication. In the example of product contamination, the organization would need to issue a special recall of the product. If using a reverse logistics service (which ensures that all recall products are removed from store shelves) would be needed, the crisis management plan would include information on triggering this service. Additionally, special press releases and media contacts would need to be made to publicize the lot numbers or other identifying information for the products that were recalled.

Situations of this kind also indicate that trusted advisors such as your organization's insurance professional and public relations professional be consulted to ensure that all appropriate steps are taken to address the crisis and to begin the repair of public trust.

Other situations which might not directly result in physical damage could damage public trust in the overall safety of the "product." When a Northwest Airlines flight overflew its Minneapolis, MN destination because of pilot inattention, Northwest Airlines' parent organization, Delta Airlines, issued all passengers on that flight a $500 coupon for future flights within days of the incident. No one was injured, but the flight was over an hour late to its destination and the air traffic controllers' inability to make contact with the pilots triggered a security alert. The pilots' authorization to fly was subsequently revoked by the federal government. Clearly in today's tight competitive environment, Northwest/Delta could not afford to have the public question the safety of flying on their aircraft.

Emergency	Initial Action	Follow-up
Cyber and IT Disruption	Follow instructions from senior management, IT and/or Security. Turn off your computer if instructed to do so.	Provide information to internal and external stakeholders regarding the situation.
Product Contamination	Take action to remove product from store shelves using reverse logistic services; contact all distributers; contact media to advise on recall of product.	Work with reverse logistics service, insurance provider and public relations professional.
Fraud	Try to determine the extent of the activity. Determine if customers' credit card information has been compromised.	Possibly bring in forensic accountant to do a complete audit. Bring criminal charges against the perpetrators. Advise customers if credit card information has been compromised.

Cyber and IT Disruption scenarios are handled most effectively when a clear set of protocols and mitigation strategies have been established in advance and practices. No two Cyber and IT disruptions are alike, but when IT staff are trained to take assertive steps to alert the organization, shut down systems and take action to remedy the situation, then confidence is preserved.

Similarly, in the case of the discovery of fraud, management must be willing to take the necessary action to uncover the source. The organization may have to undergo a forensic audit to determine the extent of the fraud. Under no circumstances should the organization punish the whistleblower.

Activating the crisis management plan in various scenarios

Plan Component	What it looks like
Initial Action Assess what needs to be done to preserve life and property. Determine who needs medical assistance and arrange for it; determine who needs other kinds of assistance; determine what must be done to secure the facilities and physical plant.	Call 911 if indicated; Evacuate the facilities if this is indicated; shelter in place if this is indicated; Send out text messages, emails, phone alerts if these are indicated. Contact the media if this is indicated. Alerting management; employees of the crisis – and possibly action such as evacuation or shelter in place
Activate Crisis Communication Plan • Designated Spokesperson	Use of Prepared Statements for • Media communications • Stakeholder communications
Dealing with the crisis: Ongoing Action steps and ongoing communication	Specific actions taken to resolve/mitigate the crisis
Resumption	Identify action steps needed to begin the process of resuming normal operations
Post-crisis debrief	Determining the source of the crisis; how to reduce the potential for a future event of that nature; What can be learned from the event and response.
Organizational modification	Take steps to modify the source of the crisis including HR action and operational action.

Crisis Management Team

The leaders of the Crisis Management Team should be known to board, employees well in advance of a crisis. Contact information for the team should be disseminated as soon as the team is formed and updated at regular intervals. Board members and employees need to know who is leading the Crisis Management Team at the time of the crisis incident.

Phone tree

As was discussed in Chapter 4, the crisis scenario may call for activating the organization's phone tree. If the organization has an 800 number, that number should be given to the board and employees in the event of an emergency, particularly if the crisis takes place after normal work hours. The number could have a recording that provides information on the nature of the crisis, alternative location of the offices, and other information that board, employees would need.

Website

The organization's website can be a source for information and also a conduit for non profits or academic institutions to accept emergency donations. The web address can be included in press releases so that the media can publicize it.

Media Relations

This section of the crisis management plan describes how to action this important part of crisis incident management. Cultivating good media relations is essential in advance of any emergency situation. The media should have the name(s) and contact information of the Designated Spokespersons. These are the "go to" individuals who can provide the media with the most accurate information at any given moment in time. In terms of reputational risk, the quality of the organization's relationship with the media is particularly important. The way in which your organization inter-acts with the media can send a message that either reinforces your organization's good name, or sends a message of disorganization and incompetence.

The Designated Spokesperson needs to activate the organiza-tion's written protocols for interacting with media representatives. These protocols should include these instructions:

- All media inquiries must be directed to the Designated Spokesperson- no exceptions.

- Consequences must be imposed, including termination, for violating the above rule. These consequences need to apply to customers as well.

- Before speaking with the media, the Spokesperson should prepare a summary statement based on confirmed facts – al-ways tell the truth.

- Determine the most appropriate way to brief board mem-bers, staff, customers and clients.

- Update the media as the situation evolves.

The importance of a good press release   As was noted in Chapter 4, prepared statements facilitate the organization's initial interac-tion with the media following the crisis/emergency. The Designat-ed Spokesperson can simply fill in the information relevant to the crisis or emergency. The public's perception of your organization is directly correlated to the credibility and professionalism that your organization presents in the quality of the prepared statement.

- Give basic facts – name of the organization, location and brief description of the organization's mission.

- The statement should have a section (that would be filled in when a crisis occurs) that describes all of the information that has been verified: What happened in very general terms ? Who was involved? When the incident/crisis/emergency occurred? Where the crisis occurred?

- Information on how to contact the organization.

- The organization's commitment to the community, its customers and its employees.

Communication with other stakeholders

As was noted in Chapter 4, your organization's crisis communication plan should also include specific communications strategies for conveying information that is necessary and sufficient to each of these stakeholder groups.

Employees Employees will need to know where to report for work, what their assignments will be if they are going to be assigned to a department outside of their normal work duties.

Clients and customers Clients and customers will want to know if their order/shipment has been affected by the crisis, where to obtain customer services, if the organization's current production schedule has been impacted by the crisis and where to call to obtain information.

Vendors Vendors need to know where the organization is operating, if organization needs a special shipment and how to get in touch with the individual(s) handling vendor inquiries.

Financial institutions Banks, stock brokerages and other financial institutions will want to know if the organization has moved to a temporary location, names of individuals who are authorized to transact business and if any board protocols on emergency financial operations have been triggered. Remember, the financial institutions will want to see prior to any crisis incident documents and authorization (such as signatures) for individuals who would be authorized to transact business during a crisis scenario. Remember, the bank or other financial institutions are limited by the organization's written instructions in terms of who is authorized to do business with the bank. Banks and financial institutions are not permitted to allow anyone within the organization to do business with the bank unless expressly authorized in writing.

Public The public information needs are more general and center on where the organization is located and the extent to which the organization's business operations have been affected by the crisis.

The Sample Scenarios

The sample scenarios represent possible events that could happen to any organization. As the chart below indicates, there are specific reputational implications for the handling or mishandling of these incidents. Each scenario will describe a recommended initial notification and crisis communications strategies.

Emergency	Reputational Risk
Fire	Employees and visitors will be injured or killed because they did not know how to evacuate the building and go to a designated safe area.
Earthquake	Employees and visitors will be injured or killed because they did not know what to do in the event of an earthquake.
Tornado or Severe Storm	Employees and visitors will be injured or killed because they did not know what to do in the event of a tornado or severe storm.
Cyber and IT Disruption	Hacking or compromise of the organization's website, IT systems, databases containing customer credit card or financial information.
Workplace violence	Employees and visitors could be injured or killed in workplace violence incident.
Product Defect or Contamination	Consumers may refuse to purchase products that they perceive to be defective or contaminated. Organizational response could restore confidence in the product.
Fraudulent Activities	Brings to light a gap in internal controls. Customer credit card or financial information may be compromised. Possible identity theft scenario.

Fire Response Plan

Any incident of a fire occurring at your organization's offices or manufacturing location will involve the local fire department, police department and possibly Emergency Medical Technicians (EMT). A fire in any building or facility may result in the loss of life or injuries, damage to physical structures, release of chemicals or biological hazards. Therefore, any suspected fire, smell of smoke, or visible manifestation of a fire should be considered as a working fire.

Initial Notification

In any situation where a fire is known to exist or if a fire is suspected, the following steps must be taken:

*   DIAL 911 AND REPORT THE FIRE
*   Contact the Chief Executive or that person's designee.
*   Sound the alarms in the affected buildings to signal the need to evacuate.
*   Activate the evacuation procedures and take a head count at the designated safe zones.

Electronic Communication Methods

Phone tree If the fire took place after hours, the phone tree would be activated to advise employees of the incident and where to report to work.

If the organization has an 800 number An 800-number could be used to advise customers about production and any delays in shipments. The number could also have several options that contained specific messages for specific stakeholder groups.

Website The organization's website can be a source for information about the fire and the location of the company, nonprofit or academic building/department's temporary location.

Crisis Communication Plan

Media Contacts Determine which media contacts would provide the most effective coverage for this event.

The importance of a good press release A prepared statement that can be used in the event of a fire should have these talking points:

- Give basic background facts – name of the organization, location and brief description of the organization's mission.

- The statement should have a section that describes (there should not be any detail until facts and circumstances can be verified):

     What happened in very general terms, *i.e. the XYZ building was destroyed/heavily damaged by fire this afternoon. Who was involved. When the fire occurred. Where the fire was located and the extent of the damage.*

- Information on how to contact the organization for customer service issues.

- The organization's commitment to the community, its customers and employees.

Communication with other stakeholders

Employees Employees would know where they needed to report for work and when.

Clients and customers The information that should be conveyed to this group includes how to contact customer service, the impact of the fire on production and/or services and where to call to obtain further information.

Vendors Vendors need to know where the organization is operating and how to get in touch with the individual(s) handling vendor inquiries.

Insurance Providers Your organization will need to contact its insurance provider and a designated adjuster.

Public Relations Professional Depending on the nature of the fire and the extent of injuries or damage, this professional would provide valuable support to the organizations' Designated Spokesperson.

Public. The press release on the fire would probably satisfy the public's need for information.

Earthquake Response Plan

Safeguarding the lives of employees is particularly important during an earthquake, since all employees are affected at the same instant. Extensive search and rescue operations may be required to locate and assist trapped or injured persons. Emergency medical care, food, and temporary shelter would be required for injured and displaced persons. Prompt action is required to calm personnel, assure them of their safety and provide care, counseling and shelter to survivors.

Initial Notification

The shaking will get your attention!! In an earthquake scenario, employees should know to drop, cover and hold on. The website for the Southern California Earthquake Center, http://www.dropcoverholdon.org/, features an interactive exercise on safety measures during an earthquake.

- Contact the Chief Executive or that person's designee.
- Sound the alarms in the affected buildings to signal the need to evacuate when the shaking has stopped and it is deemed safe to exit.
- Take a head count at the designated safe zones and advise First Responders of the names of people who are missing and where they might be in the building.

Electronic Communication Methods

Severe earthquakes often damage the areas's infrastructure including roads, telecommunications systems and other vital communication elements. A phone tree might not be feasible for several days as the local governments may request that people avoid using cell phones or land lines.

If the organization has an 800 number If possible, adding a recorded message(s) to your organization's 800 number can be an efficient way of disseminating information to customers, employees and the public. The organization's website can be a source for information. The web address can be included in the recorded message for the 800 number.

Crisis Communication Plan

In an earthquake scenario, media outlets are probably going to be concentrating on earthquake reports for the local area.

Communication with other stakeholders

Employees Employees will want to know where to report for work, when to report for work and if they are going to receive their pay on time.

Clients and Customers Clients in another part of the country or abroad need to be reassured that the organization is still functioning and has passed its administrative operations to a branch location or is able to continue operations virtually.

Vendors Vendors may or may not be available to need to fill orders or serve, but in the event that they are, they would need to know where the organization is operating and how to get in touch with the individual(s) handling vendor inquiries.

Financial institutions and other trusted advisors If the organization's bank and/or other trusted advisors are located outside of the area affected by the earthquake, the organization will want to advise them of the extent of the damage, the types of services needed and any other information that will facilitate resumption of operations.

Public. The public may inquire on the location of the organization and if the organization is still operating. This information can be provided on a recorded message on the organization's 800 number or via the organization's website.

Tornado Response Plan

Tornados are some of the most frightening displays of nature's wrath. Fortunately meteorological forecasting and modeling has made the prediction of the path and severity of a tornado more reliable. The level of destruction from a tornado can be catastrophic or minor – depending on the slightest change in the direction of the storm. Keeping everyone in your organization safe is your first priority in this scenario as there is no way to protect property from this furious storm. If your organization is located in a tornado-prone location, it is essential that everyone in the organization knows what to do in the event of this type of storm.

Tornado Watches and Warnings

When a tornado watch is announced, this means that tornadoes are expected in, or near, your area. Keep your radio or television set tuned to a local station for information and advice from your local government and the weather service. Also, keep watching the sky, especially to the south and southwest. If you see any revolving, funnel-shaped clouds, report them immediately by calling 911.

When a tornado warning is issued, it means that a tornado has actually been sighted or has been indicated by radar, and that this or other tornadoes may strike in your vicinity. Public warning will come over the radio, TV, or by five-minute steady blasts of sirens by the Civil Defense warning system.

What to do next

Once the warning is issued, then all employees and visitors must move to a safe location in the building. Take the following actions immediately:

- Get away from the perimeter of the building and exterior glass. If time permits, close drapes, blinds, etc.
- Leave your office if it is located on the building's perimeter - close the door.
- Go to the center of the building - bathrooms or stair enclosures.
- Sit down and protect yourself by putting your head as close to your lap as possible, or you may kneel while protecting your head.
- Do not use elevators and do not go to the first floor lobby or outside the building.
- Keep your radio or television set tuned to a local station for information.
- Do not use the telephone to get information or advice. This only ties up circuits.
- If you are trapped in an outside office, seek protection under a desk. Keep calm.

Electronic Communication Methods

Phone tree The aftermath of a tornado can be similar to the aftermath of an earthquake. Telephone lines and cell phone towers might be destroyed or disabled.

If the organization has an 800 number If possible, adding a recorded message(s) to your organization's 800 number can be an efficient way of disseminating information to customers, employees and the public. The organization's website can be a source for information. The web address can be included in the recorded message for the 800 number.

Crisis Communication Plan

In an tornado scenario, media outlets are probably going to be concentrating on tornado reports for the local area.

Communication with other stakeholders

Employees Employees will want to know where to report for work, when to report for work and if they are going to receive their pay on time.

Clients and Customers Clients in another part of the country or abroad need to be reassured that the organization is still functioning and has passed its administrative operations to a branch location or is able to continue operations virtually.

Vendors Vendors may or may not be available to need to fill orders or serve, but in the event that they are, they would need to know where the organization is operating and how to get in touch with the individual(s) handling vendor inquiries.

Financial institutions and other trusted advisors If the organization's bank and/or other trusted advisors are located outside of the area affected by the tornado, the organization will want to advise them of the extent of the damage, the types of services needed and any other information that will facilitate resumption of operations.

Public The public may inquire on the location of the organization and if the organization is still operating. This information can be provided on a recorded message on the organization's 800 number or via the organization's website.

IT or Cyber-Related Crisis Response

Initial Notification

The source of an initial notification for an IT or Cyber-related crisis could emerge from a number of areas including customer complaints, alerts from an employee, vendor or other stakeholder.

Crisis Management Team

The Crisis Management Team, which includes the Designated Spokesperson, would need to focus on the nature and severity of the problem and authorize the necessary actions to mitigate the crisis. Although damage assessment might not take place for hours or even days, it is essential that technology expertise be available immediately to identify those actions that need to take place immediately.

If the crisis affects customers or external stakeholders, the Designated Spokesperson will need to issue a press release. If the organization is located in a state such as California which has a law requiring that customers be notified of a real or possible breach of security involving their credit card or financial information, then customers need to be contacted individually to be apprised of the situation.

The Crisis Management Team will need to consult with the organization's insurance provider, legal counsel and public relations professional for guidance in dealing effectively with this type of crisis.

Electronic Communication Methods

Phone tree Depending on the nature of the crisis, employees may need to be advised by phone to shut down their computers. The use of a phone tree would be necessary if the crisis involved a computer virus that destroyed files and databases.

If the organization has an 800 number The organization's 800 number could have a recorded message about the crisis for customers and another for the general public.

Website If the crisis involves the hacking or compromising of the organization's website, the Crisis Team would need to be advised by their technology experts on alternative options or an alternative website link.

Crisis Communication Plan

Media Relations

The importance of a good press release   The Designated Spokesperson should work directly with the organization's public relations professional to prepared press releases for this type of incident. The statement needs to be transparent in terms of the nature of the crisis and the impact that it has had or will have on the organization, customers and the public at large. The press release should be very clear about what is being done (without disclosing proprietary information) to mitigate the crisis, how customers and other stakeholders can contact the organization and when normal operations are expected to resume. The statement should contain a statement emphasizing the organization's commitment to the community and its customers.

Media Contacts   Which media contacts would provide the most effective coverage? Depending on the organization's industry and location, local media contacts would be a good first step. If the nature of the situation requires broadcast to a larger area, then contacting regional or national media outlets may be necessary.

Communication with other stakeholders

Employees   Employees will need to know how to proceed with their duties in this situation and, if necessary, what actions to take to preserve their electronic files and databases. Employees will need to be reminded to refer all media inquiries to the Designated Spokesperson because the situation requires that only verified information be released to customers, the media and the public.

Clients and Customers   Clients will need to know if or how the crisis affects them. If the nature of the crisis involves a real or possible compromise to their financial information, then the organization needs to take steps to comply with all applicable laws relating to this type of situation.

Vendors   Vendors will need to know if the crisis affects any relevant financial information that the organization may have about the vendor's business.

Financial institutions   Banks, stock brokerages and other financial institutions will want to know the details of the crisis and how it might affect the organization's accounts with these institutions.

Public   Public inquiries need to be addressed by means of a general statement providing information on the nature of the crisis and how to contact the organization if necessary.

Workplace Violence Incident Response Plan

Workplace violence is one of the most frightening scenarios for any organization to confront. Although consultants rarely encounter truly "taboo" topics in dealing with clients, workplace violence is as close as it comes to a forbidden subject. Unfortunately in today's society, silence on this topic can indeed be deadly.

Initial Notification

The initial notification of workplace violence could be via an alarm, a coded message via the organization's intercom or, unfortunately, via the sound of gunfire or other weapon. Employees should be trained to immediately shelter-in-place in this situation and attempt to call 911 to report the incident. Depending on the situation, however, it may be safer for employees to evacuate their building. Your organization needs to determine what the best options would be in this type of scenario and develop training around specific types of signals and workplace violence scenarios.

Crisis Management Team

What would be this group's priorities in this situation? The Crisis Management Team would need to immediately ensure that 911 was called to alert police, fire and EMT personnel to the scene. Following the incident, the Team will need to ensure that all employees, visitors or others on the organization's premises receive medical treatment if necessary, and that work and production schedules have been either suspended or altered to support those affected by the scenario.

The Team will need to begin work immediately with the Designated Spokesperson and the organization's insurance provider, attorney and public relations professional. The organization should seriously consider offering counseling services to all employees.

Electronic Communication Methods

Phone tree If the scenario takes place after normal work hours or on a weekend, the use of a phone tree would be useful in advising employees about the scenario. A phone tree is not necessarily a good option to alert the employees that the scenario is taking place unless the organization has a means by which an alert message can be relayed to all telephones in the building.

If the organization has an 800 number The organization might consider putting a recorded message on its 800 number following the incident.

Website Information about the incident could be placed on the website in the context of extending condolences and assuring customers that the organization is still operating.

Crisis Communication Plan - Workplace Violence

Media Relations The Designated Spokesperson will need to work carefully with the organization's legal counsel and public relations professional to craft a press release that describes what happened in very general terms:

- Who was involved (this should be cleared through legal counsel and law enforcement)

- When and where the violence occurred (again, details need to be cleared through legal counsel and law enforcement)

- Information on how to contact the organization

- The organization's commitment to the community and its customers

Media Contacts   Which media contacts would provide the most effective coverage?

In today's era of 24/7 coverage, the media will likely be arriving at the scene either during or immediately following the incident. The organization's Designated Spokesperson should refer media inquiries at that point to law enforcement that will probably have one of their Public Information Officers (PIO) at the scene. This individual is expert at dealing with the media in situations like this.

In the days following the incident if the organization wishes to release a statement, the Designated Spokesperson with advice from the organization's public relations professional can prepare a press release.

Communication with other stakeholders

Employees   Employees will need to know what happened, if any of their colleagues were injured and, if any were killed, where to find information on memorial services. Employees will also need to know about changes in work schedule, production deadlines or location of their workplace. The organization should seriously consider offering counseling services to all employees. The information disseminated to employees should include information on accessing counseling.

Clients and Customers   Clients and customers will want to know if the organization is still open or if the hours of operation have been temporarily changed.

Vendors   Vendors need to know if the organization is operating, where to make deliveries and how to get in touch with the individual(s) handling vendor inquiries.

Financial institutions and insurance providers   These institutions will want to know if the organization is still open, if the hours of operation have been changes, how to contact the CEO, CFO or other with whom they normally interact. In the event that one of these individuals was injured or killed in the incident, they need to be told, preferably by a Board member or the Chief Executive, who will be the interim for the position. That individual may need to have a signature on file with the financial institution.

Public   Public inquiries may center on operating hours of the organization. Other inquiries which request information beyond what was made available through the media should be referred to law enforcement.

Product Defect or Contamination Response Plan

Product recalls are everyday news. The public is used to hearing that there is a recall of XYZ automobile due to problems with some part or system. The public is more sensitive to hearing about a defect or contamination in a product that is consumed or intended for children or pets. If your organization manufactures or sells these types of products, it is particularly important to have an ongoing relationship with a public relations professional and a reverse logistics firm that can be called upon to remove products from store shelves.

Initial Notification

The initial notification that a product is defective or contaminated would be a number of sources including internal inspectors or from consumers who were affected by the defect/contamination.

Crisis Management Team

The Crisis Management Team would need an immediate assessment of the extent of the defect/contamination to determine the next steps. If the defect/contamination is localized, then the product can be quickly removed from the retail outlets in that area. If the defective/contaminated products have been distributed over a wide area, the organization will need to call upon a reverse logistics firm to remove the products from the retail establishments in which they are currently located. Retailers should be alerted immediately to remove the product from store shelves and also to publicize the lot number or other identifying serial numbers of the defective/contaminated product.

The Team should begin consultation with its insurance provider, attorney and public relations professional to craft a crisis communication campaign to alert the public.

Electronic Communication Methods

Phone tree   A phone tree to alert retailers, media outlets and vendors would be useful in disseminating important information on the defective/contaminated product.

Website and 800 number   The organization's website and 800 number could be used to provide information on the description, lot/serial numbers of the products and how to return the items.

Crisis Communication Plan

Media Relations -The importance of a good press release.   The Designated Spokesperson and the organization's public relations professional would collaborate to provide an informative press release which provides the following information:

- Description and serial numbers of the product.
- How to return the product for a full refund.
- How to contact the organization – 800 number and website.
- Any other relevant information.
- The organization's commitment to the community and its customers.

Communication with other stakeholders

Employees   Employees need to be informed about the recall and if the scenario requires altered working hours and/or work location.

Clients and Customers The information provided in the press release and via the 800 number and website should suffice for the customers' immediate information needs.

Vendors Vendors would need to know if the scenario will affect orders or deliveries and how to contact the individual(s) handling vendor inquiries.

Financial institutions Banks, stock brokerages and other financial institutions will want to be apprised of the scenario and if the incident has affected the organization's current production schedule.

Public The information presented in the press release, 800 number and website should be sufficient.

Fraudulent Activities Response Plan

Discovering that fraudulent activities are taking place in your organization can be one of the most devastating revelations for any executive. Generally, the extent of the fraud takes some time to determine. Often executives, particularly in nonprofits and academic institutions, are reluctant to prosecute because of the accompanying publicity. This type of scenario calls for frank and open discussion with all of your trusted advisors. Perpetrators of fraud count on the organization's reluctance to prosecute as well as the organization's reticence in disclosing the incident to future employers of the perpetrator. Someone who is caught engaging in fraudulent activities in your organization has probably done it before and gotten away with it. Your organization will need to decide what to do to advise clients or customers if their sensitive information has been compromised. Your organization will also need to decide what it needs to do to deal with the perpetrator and what it needs to do to tighten internal controls.

Initial Notification

The initial notification that fraudulent activities have taken place can come from a variety of sources including your organization's auditor, bank or a whistleblower. [Editorial note: If the notification came from a whistleblower, consider giving this person a bonus!]

Crisis Management Team

The Crisis Management Team would need an immediate assessment of the extent of the fraud to determine the next steps. If the fraudulent activities are limited to one area of the organization's finances, then steps can be taken to limit the damage. Your organization might consider bringing in a forensic accountant to begin an audit immediately.

The Team should begin consultation with its insurance provider, attorney and public relations professional to craft a crisis communication campaign if the fraud is widespread and has affected the organization's clients or customers.

Electronic Communication Methods

Depending on the nature and extent of the fraudulent activities, your organization may want to advise employees particularly if the fraudulent activities require a change in procedures.

Crisis Communication Plan

Media Relations If the fraud involves access to customers' credit card numbers, your state may have laws requiring you to contact your customers. Depending on the specific situation, and on the advice of your insurance professional and legal counsel, you may want to contact the media.

The importance of a good press release The Designated Spokesperson, the organization's insurance professional, legal counsel and public relations professional would collaborate to draft a press release which provides the following types of information:

- Consumers' credit card information might have been compromised.
- What the organization is going to do about this development.

- What the consumer should do about this development and how the consumer can contact the organization.

- The organization's commitment to the community and its customers

Communication with other stakeholders What would the message be for each of these stakeholder groups?

Employees Employees need to be informed about the incident within the context of improving security measures and protocols.

Clients and Customers The information provided in the press release and via the 800 number and website should suffice for the customers' immediate information needs.

Vendors Vendors would need to know if the scenario will affect orders or deliveries and how to contact the individual(s) handling vendor inquiries.

Financial institutions Banks, stock brokerages and other financial institutions will want to be apprised of the scenario and the organization's plans for improved security.

Public The information presented in the press release should be sufficient.

The Value of Lessons Learned: Post-Crisis Debrief

The Crisis Management Team, the Chief Executive, and members of the Executive Committee of the Board should take part in a post-crisis debrief should take place within one or two weeks from the date of the crisis scenario. The purpose of the debrief is to review the significant aspects of the response, particularly the quality of the crisis communication response. Specifically, by the time that the debrief takes place, information should be available assessing possible damage to the organization's brand and image. If damage to the brand and image has been sustained because of the incident, then steps need to be outlined to begin the process of restoring public confidence.

Based on the response, what lessons were learned? Determine how the assessment of the response can be leveraged to improve responses to future crisis scenarios (a similar scenario or other scenarios). The debrief should also assess the quality of assistance gleaned from the organization's trusted advisors. When were they consulted? How did their support and advice assist in resolving the crisis? What other types of support/advice would have been helpful in the situation? If the organization does not feel it received the type of help and support from their current trusted advisors, then it is time to either renegotiate the relationship in terms of what the organization needs/expects from the trusted advisor, or find a new trusted advisor. It is entirely possible that the inadequate response resulted from shortcomings on both sides. The frank and honest discussion with your trusted advisor(s) can lead to much needed improvements.

Organizational modification

Take steps to modify the source of the crisis including HR action and operational action.

One of the most important outcomes from the debrief is the recognition of gaps or flaws in the organization's operations, production process, internal controls or response to a crisis. Changes may need to be made in the organizational structure, security, response protocols or production process.

Summary

When a crisis scenario is upon a company, nonprofit or academic institution, organizations that successfully weather the storm have a crisis management plan in place to effectively cope with the situation. Activating the Plan focuses on these primary elements:

- **A Crisis Management Team which includes the Designated Spokesperson.** The response to a crisis scenario must be guided by people who are recognized the rest of the organization as leaders in time of an emergency.

- **A trained, articulate Designated Spokesperson and at least one back-up spokesperson.** The Designated Spokesperson is the "face" of the company, nonprofit or academic institution. This individual's skill and credibility are key factors in establishing and maintaining a positive rapport with the visual, print and online media outlets. Having a back-up spokesperson is a must.

- **Prepared statements and press releases.** Although it is impossible to know in advance what the nature of a crisis will be, it is essential that generic prepared statements and press releases are available for immediate access in the event of an emergency. Although these statements can be easily edited to reflect the nature of the current situation, they need to be "camera ready" for publication.

- **Trusted Advisors.** The Crisis Management Team needs to work collaboratively with the organization's trusted advisors including their insurance provider, public relations professional, legal counsel and banker or financial advisor. These advisors are essential to give advice on managing the crisis and resuming normal operations.

- **Strategies for communicating with the organization's various stakeholder groups and constituencies.** The nature of any crisis or emergency means that your organization will need to provide information to various groups of people such as board members, staff, clients and vendors. The crisis communication plan needs to have a strategy in place for providing these groups with the level of information that is necessary and sufficient to their needs.

In Chapter 6 we will examine the value of training and practice as a means of testing the various scenarios in your organization's crisis management plan and introducing an important element of continuous quality improvement.

Step Three

Weaving Crisis Management Practices
into the Organizational Fabric

six

Training and Practice
Preparing To Take Action

*How your organization deals with a crisis will be
remembered long after the crisis has passed.*

How can your organization be truly prepared to deal with any crisis situation that emerges? The answer is simple: Practice, practice and practice. The primary objective in reputational risk management is to create a plan that guides the organization through any crisis in a manner that preserves life, secures property and maintains public confidence in the organization's brand and image. Despite how well crafted the plan may be, if the organization is not prepared to carry it out, the plan is worthless.

This chapter will present recommendations for training that addresses multiple layers of the organization, from a simple evacuation exercise for everyone to a more specialized approach for key organizational members such as the Chief Executive, Designated Spokesperson, Director of IT, Director of Production and the Chief of Security. Training needs to be implemented on an ongoing basis to ensure that the expectations, normative behaviors and limitations (such as referring all media inquiries to the Designated Spokesperson) are reinforced.

Introducing Training as an Ongoing Organizational Building Block

Crisis Management training is an essential building block for your organization. The better prepared your employees are to deal with emergency or crisis situations, the more confident they will be when the time comes to go into action. The organization strengthens its reputation as a competent, committed entity because it cares enough to prepare for the *inevitable*. Emergencies and crises occur routinely. Organizations that contend that it could never happen to them are simply delusional. It can happen and it will happen. Your organization can take steps to reduce the frequency and severity of emergency and crisis scenarios by recognizing and dealing with the organization's vulnerabilities – and by training everyone in the organization to respond competently to a crisis situation.

Tone at the Top

Even the most skillfully-crafted crisis management plan will not be effective if it is not championed from the very top of the organization. This means that the organization's Board and Chief Executive must clearly articulate their support for the plan. These organizational leaders must issue an explicit directive that everyone in the organization will fully participate in crisis management training and that all employees will fully comply with all of the plan's specifications, particularly the directive that all media inquiries will be directed to the Designated Spokesperson. Executive management needs to provide a brief explanation regarding the role of the Designated Spokesperson and why the nature of a crisis situation necessitates that this individual be the sole voice of the organization.

Shaping the Training and Practice Exercises to Suit the Organization's Culture

As we discussed in Chapter 1, the organization's culture describes how the organization expects employees to behave, the ways in which decisions are made and the overall profile of the organization. Having a solid understanding of the way things are done in your organization is essential when creating a training agenda and schedule of practice exercises.

Consider how the answers to the following questions would have an effect on the way training would be done in your organization.

Broadcasting Information within the Organization

- How are important ideas communicated within the organization?

- How do people communicate with each other – if they are in the same location and with colleagues/associates in other locations?

Describe the way in which important information is disseminated

- Announcements presented to a live audience?

- Announcements disseminated on email?

- Use of the organizational intranet to make announcements?

Use of technology

What types of technology are employed to communicate up and down the corporate ladder?

- Email
- Intranet
- Organization website
- Instant messaging
- Text messaging
- other

The answers to these questions illustrate the communication patterns within your organization. If your employees are used to communicating with each other via the company's email and/or intranet, then training is more likely to be successful if it is conducted via webinar, tele-seminar or via the organization's intranet.

In designing a training agenda, choose the communication patterns and communications media that are the most familiar to your employees.

Your organization may need to improve the quality of communication up and down the chain of command. If this is the case, training to improve the quality of communication patterns will be worth the investment of time and effort.

Establishing the Training Agenda

The organization's training agenda should include a description of the types of crises or emergencies that will be addressed. Although any number of scenarios can be envisioned, it is important to limit training to those types of situations that are genuinely possible. If your organization is not located in a seismically active area, then skip the training for earthquakes. Similarly, if your organization is not located in an area of the country that experiences tornados, then don't train for it.

Scenarios such as fire and workplace violence can occur anywhere. Both can be deadly if people in the organization do not know how to stay safe and follow instructions. Following instructions in an emergency scenario can be one of the most challenging things to train employees to do. However, with consistent practice, employees will come to understand that in emergency scenarios they may be asked to take action when they are frightened or traumatized. They simply need to know that the instructions are there to keep them safe. Practice, practice, practice. If possible, ask your local Fire Department if they can speak to your employees to reinforce the training you are offering.

Set up your organization's training agenda to assist the various constituencies in your organization to obtain the types of training that they need. Examples of constituencies who would benefit from specialized training include:

Receptionist staff/telephone operators. These employees will need training in referring inquiries to the Designated Spokesperson and routing calls to special customer service numbers.

Security. The organization's security staff, whether in-house or out-sourced, needs to understand their role in an emergency requiring building evacuation or shelter in place. Employees will be counting on security staff to help them stay safe.

Administrative staff. These staff members may need to be cross-trained to step in for their colleagues in the event of a large-scale disaster/emergency.

Manufacturing, Production, Sales and Customer Service staff. In the event of a crisis related to defective or contaminated products, these employees will need to be able to launch the organization's crisis management plan to alleviate the impact of the crisis.

Web-related functions, IT and website maintenance. The employees in this department will have a central role in any crisis or emergency, but mainly in those scenarios that involve hacking and the compromise of sensitive or proprietary information.

Executives. The Crisis Management Team is comprised primarily of executives and key members of staff such as the Designated Spokesperson and back-up spokespersons along with IT specialists and senior security managers . This group needs to train the most frequently and in collaboration with the organization's trusted advisors such as the public relations professional.

Board members. Although board members may or may not take an active part in crisis management, today's governance paradigm dictates that board members are responsible for knowing everything about the organization's operations. Crisis management is an important part of any organization's operations.

Sample Training Agenda

Emergency	Initial Action	Training Strategy
Fire	Alert the main desk and ensure that 911 has been contacted. Remain calm Note your location on the evacuation map Move in an orderly fashion toward the stairs and exit the building Close all doors as you exit Don't use elevators Once outside of the building, move away from the building	Building Evacuation Exercises – [scheduled X times per year] • Headcount at primary gathering site. Report names of individuals not accounted for to firefighters. • Headcount at secondary gathering site.
Earthquake	Stay calm and "Duck and Cover" Stay clear of tall objects and windows. Stay under cover until the initial shocks have subsided	Earthquake exercises [scheduled X times per year if the organization is located in seismically active region.] Duck, Cover, Hold On Meet in the designated area. Ensure that staff, clients and others in the office are accounted for. Advise emergency personnel if anyone is missing.

Emergency	Initial Action	Training Strategy
Tornado	Get away from the outside walls of the building and exterior glass. If time permits, close drapes, blinds, etc. Go to the center of the building - bathrooms or stair enclosures. Sit down and protect yourself by putting your head as close to your lap as possible, or you may kneel while protecting your head.	Tornado Shelter Exercises [scheduled X times per year if the organization is located in an active tornado region.] • Once the "all clear" signal has been sounded, meet in the designated area for a head-count. • Alert First Responders to the location of individuals who were on premises, but are missing from head count.
Cyber and IT Disruption	Follow instructions from senior management, IT and/or Security. Turn off your computer if instructed to do so.	IT and Cyber Risk specialists [scheduled X times per year] • Employees train to follow instructions from IT and Cyber Risk Specialists. • Training to access and activate files and databases stored in a secured location off-site.

Emergency	Initial Action	Training Strategy
Workplace violence	Alert the main desk or a supervisor. Take steps to shelter in place.	Training should include evacuation protocols in addition to shelter-in-place protocols. Schedule training to deal with this scenario on a semi-annual or even quarterly basis if this type of risk is perceived to be significant for the organization.
Product Contamination	Take action to remove product from store shelves using reverse logistic services; contact all distributers; contact media to advise on recall of product.	Training should include practice exercises with reverse logistics service, insurance provider and public relations professional.
Fraudulent Activities	Try to determine the extent of the activity. Determine if customers' credit card information has been compromised.	Training should emphasize methods for determining the extent of the possible fraud and contacting clients/customers if sensitive information could be compromised. Crisis communication and prepared statements should be practiced.

Reputational Risks Associated With Crisis Scenarios

Emergency	Reputational Risk	Training Strategy
Fire	Employees and visitors will be injured or killed because they did not know how to evacuate the building and go to a designated safe area.	**Building Evacuation Exercises – [scheduled X times per year]** • Practice evacuation and headcount at **primary** gathering site. Report names of individuals not accounted for to firefighters. • Practice evacuation and headcount at **secondary** gathering site.
Earthquake	Employees and visitors will be injured or killed because they did not know what to do in the event of an earthquake.	**Earthquake exercises [scheduled X times per year if the organization is located in seismically active region.]** **Practice -Duck, Cover, Roll** Meet in the designated area after the shaking stops. Ensure that staff, clients and others in the office are accounted for. Advise emergency personnel if anyone is missing.

Emergency	Reputational Risk	Training Strategy
Tornado or severe storm	Employees and visitors will be injured or killed because they did not know what to do in the event of a tornado or severe storm.	**Tornado Shelter Exercises [scheduled X times per year if the organization is located in an active tornado region.]** • Once the "all clear" signal has been sounded, meet in the designated area for a head-count. • Alert First Responders to the location of individuals who were on premises, but are missing from head count.
Cyber and IT Disruption	Hacking or compromise of the organization's website, IT systems, databases containing customer credit card or financial information.	**Training for IT and Cyber Risk specialists** **[scheduled X times per year]** • Employees need to train to act on instructions from IT and Cyber Risk Specialists. • Training to access and activate files and databases stored in a secured location off-site.

Emergency	Reputational Risk	Training Strategy
Workplace violence	Employees and visitors could be injured or killed in workplace violence incident.	**Training should include evacuation protocols in addition to shelter-in-place protocols.** Schedule training to deal with this scenario on at least a semi-annual basis. Schedule the training on a quarterly basis if this type of risk is perceived to be significant for the organization.
Product Defect or Contamination	Consumers may refuse to purchase products that they perceive to be defective or contaminated. Organizational response could restore confidence in the product.	Training should include reverse logistics to remove product from retail establishments. Training in specialized crisis communication techniques. Collaborate with reverse logistics vendor and public relations professional.
Fraudulent Activities	Consumers may sever their relations with the organization if they believe that their financial data/ credit card information has been compromised.	Training should emphasize methods for determining the extent of the possible fraud and contacting clients/customers if sensitive information could be compromised. Crisis communication and prepared statements should be practiced.

Training For Specific Senarios

Fire

Training for a fire scenario relies heavily on the evacuation protocol established when your organization prepared its crisis management plan. Be sure that everyone in your organization is trained to evacuate the building. The training should include a clear description of:

- The location of nearest emergency exits, fire extinguishers and fire alarm pull stations – on each floor of the building. Employees should know where the nearest exit is even if they are not sitting at their workstations.

- Employees should be able to know all of the evacuation routes, and assembly areas (primary and back-up) for your work site and building.

- Employees need to be trained that during an evacuation exercise, they need to evacuate the building and go directly to the designated meeting locations – not to the nearest Starbucks! The meeting areas are places for your employees to gather, STAY, be counted as part of an overall "head count" and wait for instructions or the "all clear" notification by emergency response personnel. Be sure to also conduct an evacuation exercise that requires employees to meet at alternate meeting locations.

Earthquake

Announce the exercise in advance by means of text message, email or special notice that appears on computer screens. Be specific in terms of date and time. The idea is for everyone to experience the exercise at the same time.

- **DUCK, COVER AND HOLD ON** – Employees should be trained to do this as long as the shaking continues.

- Upon hearing a designated signal, employees should then proceed to the designated evacuation meeting locations, when instructed by emergency services personnel. It is important for employees to understand that they should NOT simply evacuate the building in the event of an earthquake as debris from other buildings could be raining down.

- Employees should be able to know all of the evacuation routes, and assembly areas (primary and back-up) for your work site and building. For an earthquake exercise, employees may be directed to a meeting area other than the one used for a fire evacuation exercise. It is important for employees to **LEARN TO LISTEN AND PAY ATTENTION TO THE INSTRUCTIONS.**

- Employees need to be trained that during an evacuation exercise, they need to evacuate the building and go directly to the designated meeting locations. The meeting areas are places for your employees to gather, STAY, be counted as part of an overall "head count" and wait for instructions or the "all clear" notification by emergency response personnel. Be sure to also conduct an evacuation exercise that requires employees to meet at alternate meeting locations.

Tornado

If your organization is located in an area that is prone to tornados, you need to train your employees to listen for the way an announcement about a tornado or severe storm will be made. The organization can use a public address system, text message system, group phone calls, email or computer screen warnings to alert employees that a tornado warning has been issued for your area and that employees must now move to a safe location in the building.

Employees need to be trained to always take these actions in the event of a tornado or severe storm:

- Get away from the perimeter of the building and exterior glass. If time permits, close drapes, blinds, and other window coverings.

- Leave your office if it is located on the building's perimeter -

close the door.

- Go to the center of the building - bathrooms or stair enclosures.

- Sit down and protect yourself by putting your head as close to your lap as possible, or you may kneel while protecting your head.

- Do not use elevators and do not go to the lobby or outside the building.

- If the electricity is on keep radios tuned to a local station for information.

Do not use the telephone. This only ties up circuits. Updated information will be passed on to you via the [specify the means] as often as possible.

Cyber and Information Technology

Disruption   Training for this type of disruption should concentrate on those departments such as IT , Finance and/or other departments with the greatest concentration of databases and IT protocols. In addition to the key departments selected for this exercise, the Designated Spokesperson and the Crisis Management Team need to be actively involved in this training.

- The training should include desktop s scenarios in which a fictitious crisis scenario is described and the participants are given a relatively short (less than 60 minutes) timeframe in which to describe the response to the crisis.

- The response needs to be detailed, provide evidence that the solution will indeed properly address the nature of the crisis and describe the specific steps to be taken, key players, and impact on the organization's brand and image.

- The training might also include a mock-up of a press briefing in which the Designated Spokesperson is trained to hold a press conference on the nature of scenario. Individuals who could play the roles of reporters would be tasked with asking questions and providing a critique of the response.

Workplace Violence

Training to deal with this scenario should include teaching employees, particularly receptionists, to sound an "alert" either via a button located under their desks or through the use of a coded message on the intercom such as, "Paging Mark Smith" to alert the employees to shelter in place immediately. The alert button can trigger a signal that sounds like a doorbell or chimes rather than a siren.

Employees should be trained to know how to shelter in place even if they are not located in their own offices. This is particularly important if employees work in a large "bullpen" configuration. The workplace should have features that would allow for quick access to a safe haven. Once the alarm has been sounded, employees need to QUIETLY:

• Go to a corner or area to the left or right of the door if possible. Do NOT gather near the door or directly across from the door.

• Push a piece of furniture up against the door or take some other measure to secure the door from being pushed in from the outside.

• Depending on the workplace violence situation that triggered the order it may be necessary to maintain silence. Teaching employees to BE QUIET could be just as vital in saving their lives as teaching them to find shelter.

• If possible, quietly use a cell phone to call or better yet text message the organization's security team or 911 to advise that X number of people are located in _____room in _____building.

• Remain in the room until the all-clear signal is given.

Product Defect or Contamination

This type of training should include working with the production team, the Designated Spokesperson and the Crisis Management Team. Desktop exercises that focus on product defect or contamination scenarios should be used to train key members of the organization to take action in response to this scenario. As part of the training, the individuals in the exercise should be required to build in a plan on contacting the organization's public relations professional and reverse logistics vendor. The vendor might even be willing to collaborate with your organization in doing a joint training exercise particularly if your organization's products are distributed over a large geographic region.

The training might also benefit from a mock-up of a press briefing in which the Designated Spokesperson is trained to hold a press conference on the nature of scenario. Individuals who could play the roles of reporters would be tasked with asking questions and providing a critique of the response.

Fraudulent Activities

The training for this scenario should focus on crisis management, crisis communications and public relations. The Crisis Management Team should identify those departments within the organization that would be key in responding to this type of crisis. For example, the departments could include IT, Finance, Purchasing, Accounts Receivable, Accounts Payable and others. The training exercise should involve isolating the activity and tracking the source of the fraud –which could be external to the organization. If the fraud is being perpetrated via hackers, then the IT department should be trained routinely in shutting down the access, disabling the website and/or other portals.

Crisis communication training needs to focus specifically on determining the appropriate information to release, working with law enforcement, and notifying customers/clients if sensitive information has been compromised.

Given the ever increasing incidents of hacking and other cyber crimes, the training for this type of scenario should be at least four

(4) times a year using different scenarios for each training event.

Ongoing Training in Media Management

Reputational crises are often exacerbated because the organization does not effectively manage media interaction. The key person in dealing with the media is the Designated Spokesperson often in collaboration with the organization's public relations profession. Training can take the form of mock interviews and press conferences with individuals playing the role of broadcast media reporters using the array of crisis scenarios.

Designated Spokespersons, primary and back-up, need to train frequently on interview techniques, conducting press briefings and press conferences on the topics covered in the array of crisis scenarios that the organization has incorporated into the training agenda. The intent is to help the Designated Spokespersons become more adept in dealing with difficult situations and dealing with broadcast media reporters. If there is a college or university in your area that offers communications or drama degrees, your organization might be able to partner with them to offer this type of training. It would be a win/win as their students would have an opportunity to practice their skills in the role of a professional journalist.

Training for front-line employees to refer all media inquiries to the Designated Spokesperson

Receptionists and clerical staff need to be trained to refer all media inquiries to the designated spokespersons. Once the training is complete, the employees need to be aware that they will be tested occasionally to ensure compliance. This could be done as a "secret shopper" exercise or during an announced mock scenario.

A "secret shopper" exercise generally involves an individual playing the role of a shopper in a retail store or a guest in a hotel for the purpose of evaluating the quality of service and the employee compliance with organizational directives. In this case the "secret shopper" is an individual playing the role of a reporter from the media. The pseudo-reporter either phones into the organization or appears in the lobby. The person identifies himself/herself as a reporter from XYZ media outlet. S/he asks the receptionist a question or requests an opinion. The receptionist – or anyone else who the person talks to- is supposed to refer the inquiry to the Designate Spokesperson. Ideally, the employee says," Let me connect you with Suzy Smith or Larry Jones, our organization's Designated Spokesperson." The organization is expected to have someone available to act in this capacity at all times. So even if Suzy or Larry are away from their desks, Fred, Ginger or whoever is designated as a back-up, should be available to speak with the pseudo-reporter.

What happens when employees do not refer the inquiry to the Designated Spokesperson? The individuals who are involved should be counseled by HR and receive a copy of a memo outlining the incident and putting them on notice that progressive discipline will continue if they do not comply with the directive. The organization also needs to send a broadcast email to all employees reminding them about the expected behavior. The "secret shopper" exercises should be continued and increased in frequency so that receptionist staff becomes accustomed to referring media inquiries.

Summary

Some of the most powerful lessons Learned from Morgan Stanley and Chances for Children on September 11, 2001 include the need to train employees to cope with emergency situations. Training not only helps employees to understand the mechanics of dealing with a particular situation, but also to take action with confidence. Never underestimate the power of persistence and consistency in training. If your organization focuses on nothing else, take the time and energy to ensure that everyone in the organization – from the most senior person to the newest employee at least knows how to get out of the building, how to shelter in place and why they must refer all media inquiries to the designated spokesperson.

Step Four

Staying on Track

seven-seven-

10 Ways To
Jumpstart the Process and
Keep It Moving

Often the best way to begin planning for a reputational crisis is to simply jump right in. The process need not be cumbersome, but the planning needs to continually move ahead. Here are some methods to help forward the action.

1. **The board and executives need to make a visible commitment to the organization's crisis management plan and model the behavior needed to develop and preserve the plan.**

   The more vocal and visible the board and executives can be around crisis management, the less likely it will be dismissed as a fad by employees. Certainly in these economic times, the value proposition of preparing to respond competently to a crisis and thus preserving the organization's brand and image should be very obvious. The employees need to see how the board and executives have adopted the best practices of these types of plans and how they have changed the rewards for compliance. Planning of any sort will be ignored until and unless employees see a clear change in how things are done and what behavior is rewarded – and that there are unpleasant consequences for failing to comply. The organization's executive leadership should be the best prepared to deal with a reputational crisis, because they will be the "face" of the organization when a crisis occurs.

2. Use the generic structure presented in Chapter 4 as a framework for the first draft of your crisis management plan. You can create an effective crisis management plan regardless of the size of your organization.

Preparing the first edition of your crisis management plan is a triumph! Regard the generic structure as a means of facilitating that first step. Because good crisis management is a continuous process, your organization will see the plans grow and flourish each time they are updated. Soon the plans will reflect a customized approach that addresses your organization's specific profile.

3. When beginning to plan, recruit a Crisis Management Team that is comprised of the organization's "star players" – and make sure that this team is given very visible perks – including arranging for others to take part of their workload.

The organization's "star players" generally bring high levels of competence and enthusiasm to the table. It is particularly important for the board and Executives to trumpet the planning process as well as to visibly reward those individuals who were chosen to serve on the crisis management team. A seat on the team needs to become a plum assignment. The more status that can be accorded the team, the better. The perks do not have to be expensive –or even have a cost assigned to them. Prime parking space reserved for team members' use or permission to work at home several days a week sends an unmistakable message.

4. Identify the types of crises that would be most likely to affect the organization. Focus on the 4-7 most likely scenarios based on the vulnerabilities you identified in Chapter 3.

Preparing for a crisis response is more likely to succeed if you strategically choose the most likely types of scenarios that could occur in your region and in terms of your organization's operations.

5. Beware of the "Mozart" expectations! Only Mozart was able to write a composition perfectly without making any edits. Your organization's crisis management plan will need some revisions as time goes on which is perfectly normal.

    The planning team needs to focus on the task, but not be burdened with expectations that the plan produced in the crisis management planning session is perfect. It's never going to be perfect and it's never going to be absolutely finished. The nature of the plan's recurring steps provides ample opportunities for fine-tuning and course-correction.

    It is particularly important to ensure that the crisis management planning sessions are not bogged down with excessive analysis and "what-if" scenarios. Insist that the team focus on the task at hand. The plan that is produced at the end of the session may not be perfect or all-inclusive, but it is a step forward in addressing crisis management or business continuity issues. The emphasis should be on forwarding the action, not creating an encyclopedia.

6. There is no substitute for a team of effective Designated Spokespersons and a well-crafted Crisis Communications Plan.

    One of the first steps in preparing for a crisis is to identify a team of Designated Spokespersons. All of these people need to be receiving the same training in media relations, presentation and conducting press conferences. Your trusted advisors could be helpful in connecting you with the right trainers.

7. Establish a training agenda for employees at every level of your organization.

    Every employee in your organization needs to know, at the very least, three crisis responses.

    - How to safely evacuate the building.
    - How to shelter in place.

- Refer all media inquiries to the Designated Spokesperson

These should be the first three areas for employee training. Preparing a training agenda for the next six (6) months is a good way to jumpstart the training process.

8. **Practice, Practice, Practice**

In addition to the life and safety training such as fire drills and shelter in place exercises, your organization needs to practice, practice and practice crisis communications. The quality of your crisis communications and the credibility of your organization's Designate Spokesperson are essential to maintaining confidence in your organization. The more opportunities to practice, the more confident your employees will be in the event of an emergency.

9. **Debrief Is the Most Valuable Element in Practice – Put the Learning to Good Use.**

The best way to keep the process going is to acknowledge the accomplishments of the team at every juncture. At the end of the planning cycle, review the accomplishments and the learning that emerged from the process. Could this learning facilitate a more efficient or effective approach in the next round? Establish Milestones for Achievement in 30-90 Day increments. Schedule risk assessment at regular intervals.

10. **Keep talking about crisis management – walk the walk and talk the talk. Everyone in your organization is responsible for crisis management. Keep the topic in front of the whole staff.**

Keeping crisis management in front of the organization is an effective way to incorporate this planning into the organization's organizational culture. Your organization can have an excellent infrastructure regardless of its size, its age, or its budget. Your organization is an important part of your community. Crisis management is nourishment for your organization- these plans grow strong internal controls and give the organization the stamina to weather any adversity.

Some Final Thoughts

Reputational risk management is an ongoing endeavor. Hopefully the book has helped readers to become more aware of the issues central to an organization's reputation, brand and image. As you can see, any organization's reputation can be as fragile as a piece of fine crystal. Once the crystal is broken, it is almost impossible to make it whole again. Many organizations that have experienced serious reputational crises will indeed become strong again, but others will fade into history. The difference is in the level of preparation and the quality of the execution of their crisis management plans.

Keeping the Plan alive means always keeping it in front of your employees. Routine exercises to deal with emergency situations should be integrated into daily operations. Emails on emergency preparedness and safety should be broadcast on at least a monthly basis. Ongoing exercises should be scheduled on a rotating basis throughout each department in your organization. Leverage the organization's webpage and intranet to remind employees about communication patterns such as a phone tree and the update of training exercises such as those for IT and production.

If your organization routinely sponsors nonprofit organizations or partners with other organizations within your industry, consider using your Plan to assess the reputational risk that association with others such as organizations could present. Be constantly aware that reputational crises can emerge from many, many different sources. The more your organization trains to deal with a crisis, the more confident management and employees will be when they are asked to take action in a genuine crisis scenario.

How well you deal with a crisis will be remembered long after the crisis has passed.

-Selected Bibliography-

Bookkeeper Admits Embezzling From Danielle Steel, www.cbs5.com, September 28, 2009.

Brown, Ken and Dugan, Ianthe Jeanne, Arthur Andersen's Fall From Grace Is a Sad Tale of Greed and Miscues, The Wall Street Journal online, June 7, 2002, http://online.wsj.com/article/ 0,,SB1023409436545200.djm,00.html

Chronicle of Higher Education, University of California, Under Pressure, Hires Auditor for San Francisco Campus, December 8, 2009.

Clifford, Stephanie, Video Prank at Domino's Taints Brand, New York Times, April 16, 2009.

CNN Larry King Live, November 16, 2001.

Frieden, Terry, ACORN Announces New Training, Review after 'Prostitution' videos. CNN online, September 16, 2009, http://www.cnn. com/2009/US/09/16/us.acorn/index.html

Hagerty, James R., Bank Pulls Back from ACORN Work, The Wall Street Journal online, September 28, 2009, http://online.wsj.com/article/ SB125409478511144963.html.

Hoge, Patrick, Fraud Suspected at Watchdog Group, San Francisco Chronicle online, April 21, 2004, http://www.sfgate.com/cgi-bin/article. cgi?f=/c/a/2004/04/21/BAGH568BM11.DTL.

Horovitz, Bruce, Domino's Nightmare Holds Lessons for Marketers, USA Today online, April 16, 2009 http://www.usatoday.com/money/in- dustries/food/2009-04-15-kitchen-pr-dominos-pizza_N.htm.

Jackson, Peggy, Sarbanes-Oxley for Small Businesses: Leveraging Compliance for Maximum Advantage, John Wiley & Sons, New York, NY, 2006.

Jackson, Peggy, Sarbanes-Oxley for Nonprofit Boards, John Wiley &

Sons, New York, NY, 2006.

Jackson, Peggy, Done in a Day Risk Management and Business Continuity Planning, John Wiley & Sons, New York, NY,2006.

Jackson, Peggy, Sarbanes-Oxley and Nonprofit Management: Skills, Techniques, Methods, co-authored with Toni E. Fogarty, Ph.D. John Wiley & Sons, New York, NY, 2006.

Jackson, Peggy, Sarbanes-Oxley and Nonprofits: A Guide to Building Competitive Advantage, co-authored with Toni E. Fogarty, Ph.D. John Wiley & Sons, New York, NY, 2005.

Johnson, Chip, Watching the Police's Watchdogs, San Francisco Chronicle online, August 13, 2004, http://sfgate.com/cgi-bin/article. cgi?f=/c/a/2004/08/13/BAGAP87HEL1.DTL.

Kinzie, Susan, ACORN Losing Funding From Big Foundations, The Washington Post online, October 3, 2009, http://www.washingtonpost.com/wp-dyn/content/article/2009/10/02/ AR2009100205261.html.

Leonnig, Carol D., ACORN Funded Political, For-Profit Efforts, Data Show, The Washington Post online, September 25, 2009, http://www.washingtonpost.com/wp-dyn/content/article/2009/09/24/ AR2009092404775.html.

Merchant, Nomaan, Acorn CEO: Block on Federal Money 'Unconstitutional, Wrong', The Wall Street Journal, September 25, 2009, http:// blogs.wsj.com/washwire/2009/09/25/acorn-ceo-block-on-federal-money- unconstitutional-wrong.

Milbank, Dana, The Forest, the Trees and ACORN, The Washington Post online, October 7, 2009, http://www.washingtonpost.com/wp-dyn/content/article/2009/10/06/ AR2009100603098.html.

O'Keefe, Ed, Workers' Porn Surfing Rampant at Federal Agency, The Washington Post online, September 29, 2009, http://voices.washingtonpost.com/federal-eye/2009/09/eye_opener_sept_29_2009.html

Robertson, Campbell, Amount Embezzled form ACORN is Disputed, The New York Times online, October 6, 2009, http://www.nytimes.com/2009/10/06/us/06acorn.html?_r=1&scp=5&sq=%22Campbell%20Robertson%22&st=cse.

Schein, Edgar, Organizational Culture and Leadership, 2nd Ed. Jossey-Bass Publishers, San Francisco, CA. 1992.

Thomas, Cathy Booth and Fowler, Deborah, Called to Account, Time Magazine online, June 18, 2002, http://www.time.com/time/magazine/article/0,9171,1002709,00.html.

Tucker, Jill, San Francisco Schools Head Uses District Credit As Own, San Francisco Chronicle online, October 4, 2009, http://www.sfgate.com/cgi-bin/article.cgi?f=/c/a/2009/10/04/MN-7R19QQC4.DTL.

Virginia Tech Review Panel, Mass Shootings at Virginia Tech, April 16, 2007, Report of the Virginia Tech Review Panel, Presented to Timothy M. Kaine, Governor of the Commonwealth of Virginia, August 2007.

Other Books by Peg Jackson

available at:

www.pegjackson.com

www.Amazon.com

www.wiley.com

Sarbanes-Oxley for Small Businesses: Leveraging Compliance for Maximum Advantage - 978-0471998259

Sarbanes-Oxley for Nonprofit Boards: A New Governance Paradigm - ISBN: 978-0471790372

Sarbanes-Oxley for Nonprofits: A Guide to Building Competitive Advantage - ISBN: 978-0471697886

Nonprofit Risk Management & Contingency Planning: Done in a Day Strategies - ISBN: 978-0471790365

Sarbanes-Oxley and Nonprofit Management: Skills, Techniques, and Methods - ISBN: 978-0471754190

Nonprofit Strategic Planning: Leveraging Sarbanes-Oxley Best Practices - ISBN: 978-0470-12076-7

Peggy M. Jackson DPA, CPCU
6300 Stevenson Ave #403
Alexandria, VA 22304

Peggy M. Jackson, DPA, CPCU, is an author, consultant, and nationally recognized lecturer in risk management, business continuity planning, and Sarbanes-Oxley compliance. She is a Principal with Peg Jackson & Associates in San Francisco, CA and Alexandria, VA. Her specialty areas include Done in a Day® risk management and business resiliency planning. Dr. Jackson has written or coauthored seven books on risk management, business resiliency planning, and Sarbanes-Oxley compliance for nonprofit and small business audiences for publisher John Wiley & Sons. Her books, *Sarbanes-Oxley for Nonprofits* and *Risk Management and Contingency Planning: Done in a Day Strategies* won honorable mention at the 2007 Nonprofit Management Association Book Awards.

Dr. Jackson earned a doctorate in public administration (DPA) from Golden Gate University in San Francisco and holds the professional designation of Chartered Property and Casualty Underwriter (CPCU). She was recently appointed to the Governing Committee of the CPCU (national) Risk Management Interest Group. She designed the Jackson Risk Management Model© as part of an award-winning doctoral dissertation on risk management techniques. She is a member of the Washington DC Chapter of the CPCU Society and the Junior League of Washington.

www.ingramcontent.com/pod-product-compliance
Lightning Source LLC
Chambersburg PA
CBHW031810190326
41518CB00006B/274